5TH GRADE at HOME

A STUDENT AND PARENT GUIDE
with Lessons and Activities to Support 5th Grade Learning

The Staff of The Princeton Review

PrincetonReview.com

Penguin
Random
House

The Princeton Review
110 East 42nd Street, 7th Floor
New York, NY 10017

Published in the United States by Penguin Random
House LLC, New York, and in Canada by Random House
of Canada, a division of Penguin Random House Ltd.,
Toronto.

ISBN: 978-0-593-45032-1
eBook ISBN: 978-0-593-45034-5
ISSN: 2766-2365

The Princeton Review is not affiliated with Princeton
University.

Editor: Selena Coppock
Production Editors: Lyssa Mandel and
                    Emily Epstein White
Production Artist: Deborah Weber

Printed in the United States of America.

10   9   8   7   6   5   4   3   2   1

First Edition

The Editor would like to thank the Content Developer for
5th Grade at Home and *6th Grade at Home,* Mr. Patrick
Brady, for his hard work on these two titles. He jumped
into the project with tons of ideas, expertise, and
imagination, and never stopped helping out and
contributing throughout the workflow.

Editorial

Rob Franek, Editor-in-Chief
David Soto, Director of Content Development
Stephen Koch, Student Survey Manager
Deborah Weber, Director of Production
Gabriel Berlin, Production Design Manager
Selena Coppock, Director of Editorial
Aaron Riccio, Senior Editor
Meave Shelton, Senior Editor
Chris Chimera, Editor
Anna Goodlett, Editor
Eleanor Green, Editor
Orion McBean, Editor
Patricia Murphy, Editorial Assistant

Random House Publishing Team

Tom Russell, VP, Publisher
Alison Stoltzfus, Publishing Director
Ellen Reed, Production Manager
Amanda Yee, Associate Managing Editor
Suzanne Lee, Designer

For customer service, please contact
editorialsupport@review.com,
and be sure to include:

- full title of the book

- ISBN

- page number

CONTENTS

(139) Math

All About Numbers

Working with Numbers

Math in Real Life

Introduction

You and Your Child

Your job is to help your child excel in school. Everyone agrees that children bloom when their parents, family, friends, and neighbors nudge them to learn—from the Department of Education to the Parent Teacher Association, from research organizations known as "educational laboratories" to the local newspaper, from the National Endowment for the Arts to kids' shows on TV.

But state standards hardly make for enjoyable leisure reading, and plowing through reports on the best ways to teach math and reading can leave you rubbing your temples. You're caught in the middle: you want to help your child, but it's not always easy to know how.

That's where *5th Grade at Home* comes in. We identified the core skills that fifth graders need to know. Then, we put them together along with some helpful tips for you and fun activities for your child. We built this book to be user friendly, so you and your child can fit in some quality time, even as you're juggling all your other parental responsibilities.

For a helpful orientation to *5th Grade at Home*, head over to The Princeton Review's channel at www.YouTube.com/ThePrincetonReview.

Rob Franek, Editor-in-Chief of The Princeton Review, will share suggestions for how best to use these books with your child and get the most out of this educational tool. Our team at The Princeton Review is here to help you and your child as best we can.

A Parent's Many Hats

As a parent, we understand you are expected to wear many hats. Check out the following ways you can use *5th Grade at Home* to get more involved in your child's academic life.

Teacher. You taught your child how to cross the street and tie his or her shoes. In addition, you may have worked to teach your child academic skills by reviewing the alphabet, helping your child memorize facts, and explaining concepts to your child. By doing so, you are modeling a great learning attitude and great study habits for your child. You are teaching him or her the value of school.

Nurturer. As a nurturer, you're always there to support your child through tough times, celebrate your child's successes, and give your child rules and limits. You encourage your child while holding high expectations. All of this can help your child feel safe and supported enough to face challenges and opportunities at school, like new classmates, new teachers, and so on.

Intermediary. You're your child's first representative in the world. You're the main go-between and communicator for your child (school-to-home and home-to-school).

Advocate. As an advocate, you can do many things: sit on advisory councils at school, assist in the classroom, join the PTA, volunteer in school programs, vote in school board elections, and argue for learning standards and approaches you believe in.

· · · · · · · · · · · · · ●

Sometimes it's hard to know what to do, and it's easy to feel overwhelmed. But remember, it's not all on your shoulders. Research shows that family and close friends all have a huge effect on children's academic success.

What's in This Book

The Skill

Each lesson targets a key fifth-grade skill. You and your child can either work on all the lessons or pick and choose the lessons you want. If time is short, your child can work on an activity without reviewing an entire lesson.

First Things First

This is the starting point for your child in every lesson.

Parent's Corner

At the start of each chapter, we address you, the parent, and contextualize the lesson so that you can help your child. We'll share ideas, potential roadblocks, and things to watch out for.

Nouns

Nouns are words that define a person, place, or thing. Keep in mind that *thing* is a general word that includes objects, living creatures, and ideas.

Nouns can serve many different functions in a sentence. Before learning about the many uses of nouns and how nouns work with other parts of speech in a sentence, it's important to review the basics forms and types of nouns.

At the end of this lesson, you will be able to:

- understand what nouns do
- understand the difference between common nouns and proper nouns
- understand the difference between singular nouns and plural nouns
- spell and use plural nouns correctly
- understand and use possessive nouns correctly.

 Parent's Corner

You can have a lot of fun with nouns in the home. Check your fifth grader's understanding of nouns by asking them to point to nouns in your home, or quizzing them by asking if certain words are in fact nouns.

Dive Right In!

These are questions or activities for your child to complete independently. Give your child as much time as he or she needs. But if your child takes more than 30 minutes, consider the possibility that they may be having a hard time focusing, be unfamiliar with the skill, or have difficulty with the skill.

 ## Dive Right In!

Possessive Form

Directions: Fill in the possessive forms of the listed nouns.

1. Mother _____

2. Bird _____

Explore

Explore

This is where your child can go deeper into the content of the lesson. This section may include explanations, examples, and sample problems. This is what you might call the "meat and potatoes" of the lesson.

Explore

Plural Nouns to Memorize

Not all nouns follow these rules, however. There are some exceptions that must be memorized.

For some nouns that end in *f* or *fe*, you must change the *f* or *fe* to *v* and then add *-es*. In the following sentences, fill in the blank with the appropriate plural noun.

6. You took one *half*, but I wanted both _____.

7. I picked up one *leaf*, but my sister picked up an armful of
    _____

Participate

Fun, educational activities your child can do with you, family, neighbors, babysitters, and friends at home, in the car, during errands—anywhere.

Activities

These may be Hands-On Activities or In-Book Activities. They are an opportunity for your child to try out what he or she has just learned.

Participate

Activity 1: Name that Noun

Directions: Reread your journal entry. Find the nouns in your writing and categorize them here. Keep in mind that some nouns can fit into two categories! For example, in the phrase "my neighbors' homes," neighbors' is a common, plural, possessive noun. Answers will vary.

1. Did you use any common nouns? List them.

2. Did you use any proper nouns? List them.

Activity 2: Hands-On

Get a sheet of paper and look around your house to make a list of nouns that you see. Remember, a noun is a person, place, or thing. So, people can be parents, siblings, or pets, a place can be a bedroom, kitchen, and a thing can be a book, a chair, etc.

One More Thing...

These items are useful tips or facts to keep in mind, or interesting tidbits that are related to the lesson.

 ONE MORE THING... Nouns are one of the basic building blocks of the English language. Using them properly is one of the first steps in showing you have a good command of the language. How you use common versus proper nouns isn't simply a matter of rules. It is often a matter of respect. When you call your friends by name, you are talking only to them, not to people in general. Capitalizing the first letter of any proper noun shows this respect and helps proper nouns stand out in a sentence.

"My teacher, Ms. Lucille Petronio, is possibly one of the most intelligent people I know."

In a Nutshell

This is where we review the chapter content. The bullets here will echo the bullets on the front page: this contains the crucial takeaways from this chapter.

 In a Nutshell

Skills

- **Nouns** are words that define a person, place, or thing.
- **Proper noun**s are names and must be capitalized.
- **Common nouns** are not individually named and are not capitalized.
- **Singular nouns** name one person, place, or thing. Plural nouns name two or more.
- Most **plural nouns** are formed simply by adding the letter s at the end; however, there are exceptions.
- **Possessive nouns** demonstrate ownership or possession.
- For a singular noun or plural noun that does not end in s, add 's to make it possessive.
- For a plural noun that ends in s, just add the apostrophe.

Answers

You and your child can check the answers to the Dive Right In! activities and in-chapter activities. If a question or activity is extremely open-ended, it may not have a specific answer that is "correct." Feel free to discuss the answer with your child and learn how he/she came to that conclusion.

 Answers for Dive Right In:

1. Mother's
2. Bird's
3. Teacher's
4. Man's
5. Men's
6. Writers'
7. Girl's
8. Girls'

(A) Answers for Explore:

1. boxes
2. dishes
3. melodies
4. bunnies
5. essays
6. halves
7. leaves
8. team's

How Does Your Child Learn Best?

Did you know that your child learns in a lot of different ways? When children learn, they use their minds, their bodies, and their senses—their sense of sight, sound, taste, touch, and smell.

Some children can succeed in any classroom while others need specialized learning support, but all of them have strengths and weaknesses. Your child can learn to rely on his or her strengths and then work on any weaknesses. This book is full of activities that address each of these learning styles.

Visually—Using Our Sense of Sight Your child may learn best by looking at pictures, outlines, maps, and such. Your child may like to draw pictures or take notes.

Auditory—Using Our Sense of Sound Your child may learn best by listening to teachers speak, discussing with friends and classmates, or listening to music while studying. Your child may like to tap a rhythm with his or her pen or pencil while studying.

Kinesthetic—Using Our Sense of Touch and Movement Your child may learn best by moving, taking action, or walking around.

How to Use Learning Styles

Talk with your child about his or her successes at school, home, or with hobbies. How did your child learn what he or she needed to succeed? Knowing how your child learns best can help you make the most of your child's natural strengths and work on your child's weaknesses.

Once you know how your child likes to learn, you can make sure your child includes those learning methods that work (especially when studying for important tests). You can also support your child as he or she tries out more challenging learning methods. In the long run, this will help your child become a well-rounded learner!

 **The Goal**

You know getting involved with your child's school experiences is the right decision. But here's a reminder of some of the rewards you may reap! Research shows that getting involved in your child's school experiences can result in:

- Increased academic performance

- Better behavior at school

- Increased academic motivation

- Better school attendance

And lest you think your child reaps all the rewards, you might find that helping your child learn gives you:

- More info about your child's school

- A greater sense of your own learning preferences

- More appreciation for all the work you did as a student

- A better relationship with your child's teacher and school staff

Want to Know More?

Check out these online resources for more reading and math support.

Math Chimp. If you want information about more effectively helping your child in mathematics, go to http://www.mathchimp.com.

Early Math from PBS Parents. If you want activities to become more engaged in your child's school mathematics program, go to https://www.pbs.org/parents/learn-grow/all-ages/math.

Parent Resources from Reading Rockets. If you want to better understand how to enhance parent-teacher conferences and relationships, go to https://www.readingrockets.org.

Office of Elementary & Secondary Education (OESE). If you want information about training, advocates, or other educational assistance, go to https://oese.ed.gov.

Parents for Public Schools. If you want to find out about chapters of parents working together to advocate for school improvement, go to www.parents4publicschools.org.

Parent Teacher Association (PTA). If you want to connect with other parents involved in local schools, go to www.pta.org.

Parent Training and Information Centers. If you want to find out about education and services to assist a child with disabilities, go to www.parentcenterhub.org/.

Reading Is Fundamental. If you want help with supporting your child's reading and learning, go to www.rif.org.

English

Grammar & Vocabulary
Reading
Writing

Subject and Predicate

A sentence is a group of words that expresses a complete thought. Every complete sentence contains two parts: a **subject** and a **predicate**. The subject is what (or whom) the sentence is about, and the predicate states what the subject is doing or more information about the subject.

At the end of this lesson, you will be able to:

- understand what subjects and predicates do

- find subjects and predicates in text

- figure out if a group of words is a complete sentence or fragment

- write sentences using subjects and predicates correctly

Parent's Corner

One way you can help your fifth grader with this lesson is really driving home what a "subject" is. Check that they understand the difference between the *topic* (or subject!) of a sentence and the grammatical *subject* (i.e. who or what is doing the action), as students sometimes confuse the two ideas.

Dive Right In!

Writing a Journal Entry

If you were an adventurer, what kind of place would you explore?

_____

_____

_____

_____

_____

_____

_____

_____

_____

_____

_____

_____

Subject Your Journal to Review

Directions: Reread your journal entry. Circle the subjects and underline the predicates. Then answer the following questions. Answers will vary.

1. Are any sentences missing a subject or a predicate?

    _____

2. Rewrite them below as complete sentences by adding the missing parts.

    _____

    _____

    _____

    _____

    _____

    _____

    _____

    _____

    _____

    _____

    _____

    _____

    _____

    _____

Explore

Subject

The **subject** of a sentence tells whom or what the sentence is about. Circle the subject in this sentence.

1. The explorer ran from the tigress.

This sentence is about the explorer, so *the explorer* is the subject of the sentence. Often, but not always, the subject of the sentence comes before the predicate. Let's take a look at another sentence. Circle the subject in this sentence.

2. The focused tigress raced after her two-legged prey.

Whereas the subject of the last sentence was *the explorer*, the subject of this sentence is *the focused tigress*. Remember, the subject is what or whom the sentence is about. The subject is who is doing the action.

Predicate

The **predicate** tells you what the subject is or what the subject does. Now underline the predicate in the sentence about *the focused tigress.*

3. The focused tigress raced after her two-legged prey.

Ask yourself, what did the focused tigress do or be?

The focused tigress raced after her two-legged prey, so *raced after her two-legged prey* is the predicate. What happens if we add to the sentence that *the focused tigress* also does something else?

4. The focused tigress raced after her two-legged prey and caught it seconds later.

We made the predicate longer. Therefore, the predicate lengthens to become *raced after her two-legged prey and caught it seconds later.*

To express a complete thought, you need to write a complete sentence. Complete sentences contain both a subject and a predicate because each one depends on the other to make sense. Imagine trying to start a conversation without using both in a sentence.

"Is winning the game."

"After going to school."

"Went to the doctor."

"The girl with the brown hair."

"I."

These "sentences" don't make any sense! They do not have both a subject and a predicate. Therefore, they're not whole sentences; they're just fragments.

# Participate

Activity 1: Fill in the Story

Directions: Write a story with a sibling, parent, grandparent, or friend in the space below. Take turns writing the predicate of one sentence followed by the subject of the next. Answers will vary.

Once upon a time, I _____ .

predicate

_____   _____ .

subject   predicate

_____   _____ .

subject   predicate

_____   _____ .

subject   predicate

_____   _____ .

subject   predicate

_____   _____ .

    subject   predicate

_____   _____ .

    subject   predicate

_____   _____ .

    subject   predicate

_____   _____ .

    subject   predicate

_____   _____ .

    subject   predicate

_____   _____ .

    subject   predicate

_____   _____ .

    subject   predicate

Activity 2: Hands-On

On paper, write out subject and predicate, then actually draw subject and predicate examples as little cartoons.

Examples: A bear is flying a kite.

That fish is wearing a hat.

My father is mowing the lawn.

Now it's your turn.

In a Nutshell

Skills

- The **subject** of a sentence tells whom or what the sentence is about.

- The **predicate** tells you what the subject is or what the subject does.

Nouns

Nouns are words that define a person, place, or thing. Keep in mind that *thing* is a general word that includes objects, living creatures, and ideas.

Nouns can serve many different functions in a sentence. Before learning about the many uses of nouns and how nouns work with other parts of speech in a sentence, it's important to review the basic forms and types of nouns.

At the end of this lesson, you will be able to:

- understand what nouns do

- understand the difference between common nouns and proper nouns

- understand the difference between singular nouns and plural nouns

- spell and use plural nouns correctly

- understand and use possessive nouns correctly.

Parent's Corner

You can have a lot of fun with nouns in the home. Check your fifth grader's understanding of nouns by asking them to point to nouns in your home, or quizzing them by asking if certain words are in fact nouns.

Dive Right In!

Possessive Form

Directions: Fill in the possessive forms of the listed nouns.

1. Mother _____

2. Bird _____

3. Teacher _____

4. Man _____

5. Men _____

6. Writers _____

7. Girl _____

8. Girls _____

9. Child _____

10. Children _____

Answers can be found on page 30.

Explore

Proper & Common Nouns

Proper nouns are names and must be capitalized. For example, George Washington, Batman, and Finland are all proper nouns. If a noun is not naming any particular person, pet, place, or organization, then it is a **common noun** and is not capitalized.

Singular & Plural Nouns

Singular nouns name one person, place, or thing. For example, take this *hot dog* to your *friend* in the *stadium*.

Plural nouns name two or more persons, places, or things. To make most nouns plural, simply add the letter *s*. For example, take these *hot dogs* to your *friends* in the *stadiums*. However, some nouns defy the "add an *s*" rule.

To create the plural form of nouns that end in *x, sh, ch, s,* or *ss,* add *-es*. Fill in the blank in the following sentence with the appropriate plural noun.

1. One *box* of junk turns into eight _____ of junk.

2. One dirty *dish* turns into a sink full of dirty _____.

If the noun ends in a **consonant** followed by *y*, change the *y* to *i* and add -*es* to create the plural form.

3.   One irritating *melody* turns into two irritating _____.

4.   In a magic show, a gray *bunny* turns into seven gray _____.

If a noun ends in a **vowel** followed by a *y*, just add *s* to make the plural form.

5.   One great *essay* turns into many great _____.

Plural Nouns to Memorize

Not all nouns follow these rules, however. There are some exceptions that must be memorized.

For some nouns that end in *f* or *fe*, you must change the *f* or *fe* to *v* and then add -*es*. In the following sentences, fill in the blank with the appropriate plural noun.

6.   You took one *half*, but I wanted both _____.

7.   I picked up one *leaf*, but my sister picked up an armful of _____.

Other nouns change their spelling when you make them plural, so they too must be memorized. Here are some examples. Fill in the chart with the plurals.

child	
woman	
man	
alumnus	
tooth	
mouse	
goose	

Some nouns don't change at all. Fill in this chart with the plurals.

moose	
deer	
sheep	

Answers can be found on page 30.

Possessive Nouns

Possessive nouns demonstrate ownership or possession. For a singular noun or a plural noun that does not end in *s*, add *'s* to make it possessive. For a plural noun that ends in *s*, add just the apostrophe.

8. If the private jet belongs to the baseball team, then it is the

    _____ jet.

9. If the convertibles belong to the actresses, then they are the

    _____ convertibles.

ONE MORE THING... Nouns are one of the basic building blocks of the English language. Using them properly is one of the first steps in showing you have a good command of the language. How you use common versus proper nouns isn't simply a matter of rules. It is often a matter of respect. When you call your friends by name, you are talking only to them, not to people in general. Capitalizing the first letter of any proper noun shows this respect and helps proper nouns stand out in a sentence.

"My teacher, Ms. Lucille Petronio, is possibly one of the most intelligent people I know."

Participate

Activity 1: Name that Noun

Directions: Reread your journal entry from the previous chapter. Find the nouns in your writing and categorize them here. Keep in mind that some nouns can fit into two categories! For example, in the phrase "my neighbors' homes," neighbors' is a common, plural, possessive noun. Answers will vary.

1.   Did you use any common nouns? List them.

2.   Did you use any proper nouns? List them.

3.   Did you use any singular nouns? List them.

4.   Did you use any plural nouns? List them.

5.   Did you use any possessive nouns? List them.

Activity 2: Hands-On

Get a sheet of paper and look around your house to make a list of nouns that you see. Remember, a noun is a person, place, or thing. So, people can be parents, siblings, or pets, a place can be a bedroom, kitchen, and a thing can be a book, a chair, etc.

Activity 3: Hands-On

Find a magazine or newspaper in the house. On one page, find all of the nouns on that page and circle them (if permitted by your adult). Count how many nouns you found on one page.

In a Nutshell

Skills

- **Nouns** are words that define a person, place, or thing.

- **Proper nouns** are names and must be capitalized.

- **Common nouns** are not individually named and are not capitalized.

- **Singular nouns** name one person, place, or thing. Plural nouns name two or more.

- Most **plural nouns** are formed simply by adding the letter *s* at the end; however, there are exceptions.

- **Possessive nouns** demonstrate ownership or possession.

- For a singular noun or plural noun that does not end in *s*, add 's to make it possessive.

- For a plural noun that ends in s, just add the apostrophe.

Answers for Dive Right In:

1. Mother's
2. Bird's
3. Teacher's
4. Man's
5. Men's
6. Writers'
7. Girl's
8. Girls'
9. Child's
10. Children's

 Answers for Explore:

1. boxes
2. dishes
3. melodies
4. bunnies
5. essays
6. halves
7. leaves
8. team's
9. actresses'

Top Chart (page 25)

child: children

woman: women

man: men

alumnus: alumni

tooth: teeth

mouse: mice

goose: geese

Bottom Chart (page 25)

moose: moose

deer: deer

sheep: sheep

Pronouns

A **pronoun** is a word that replaces a noun (person, place, or thing). For example, *Takeshi locked Takeshi's keys in the car* becomes *He locked his keys in the car.*

At the end of this lesson, you will be able to:

- understand what personal pronouns do
- understand what interrogative pronouns do
- find pronouns in text
- figure out which noun a pronoun replaces
- write sentences using pronouns correctly

Parent's Corner

Make a list of all the people in your immediate or extended family and challenge your fifth grader to generate each person's pronouns. Make sure to correct your fifth grader if they make a mistake with pronouns in speech or writing. It is important to get these small words right!

Dive Right In!

Pronoun Types

Directions: With a sibling, parent, adult, or friend, write sentences for each type of pronoun in the chart. Underline the pronoun in each of your sentences. Answers will vary.

	Subject Pronoun	Object Pronoun	Possessive Pronoun
What It Does	*replaces the noun doing the action*	*replaces the noun receiving the action*	*replaces the noun being owned*
Singular			
Plural			
Interrogative (singular or plural)			

Explore

Personal Pronouns

A **personal pronoun** replaces a person or thing. It is less specific than the noun that it replaces, but it can do all the things nouns can do. Take a look at this sentence.

⇨ *Joy* bakes delicious cookies.

In this sentence, *Joy* is the subject because she is doing the action. In the next sentence, a personal pronoun replaces the subject noun.

She bakes delicious cookies.

To see a list of all of the **subject pronouns,** look in the first column of the chart on the next page.

Not all nouns do the action in a sentence. Some nouns receive the action.

⇨ The soccer player kicked *the ball.*

The soccer player is doing the action of kicking, but *the ball* is being kicked. Therefore, *the ball* is receiving the action. Nouns that receive actions are called objects and are replaced by **object pronouns.**

The soccer player kicked *it.*

All of the object pronouns are in the second column of the chart.

Some nouns show possession.

⇨   The laptop is *Damian's.*

Damian's is a possessive noun and tells us that Damian owns the laptop. Possessive nouns are replaced by **possessive pronouns**, listed in the last column of the chart. Replace *Damian's* with a possessive pronoun.

The laptop is _____.

	Subject Pronoun	Object Pronoun	Possessive Pronoun
What It Does	*replaces the noun doing the action*	*replaces the noun receiving the action*	*replaces the noun being owned*
Singular	I	me	mine
	you	you	yours
	he	him	his
	she	her	hers
	it	it	its
Plural	we	us	ours
	you	you	yours
	they	them	theirs
Interrogative (singular or plural)	who	whom	whose

Interrogative Pronouns

An **interrogative pronoun** replaces a person or thing that is not known. It usually appears in a question. The bottom row of the chart on the previous page shows three interrogative pronouns that are often misused: *who, whom,* and *whose.* Other interrogative pronouns that do not appear on the chart are *what, when, which,* and *where.*

	Subject Pronoun	Object Pronoun	Possessive Pronoun
Interrogative (singular or plural)	who	whom	whose

Circle the pronouns in these sentences:

1. Who got stuck in the bathtub?

2. When did this happen?

3. Where is the car parked?

Who vs. Whom

Notice on the chart that *who* is in the subject pronoun column, just like *he. Whom* is in the object pronoun column, just like *him.* If you're not sure whether to use *who* or *whom,* instead answer the question using *he* or *him.* For example, "With who/whom did you go on a date with last night?" Answer the question: "I went with him." If your answer is *him,* the correct question word is *whom.* If your answer is *he,* then the correct question word is *who.*

4. You went to the movies with (he/him) last night.

5. With (who / whom) did you go to the movies?

Whose vs. Who's

In the chart on the previous page, *whose* is in the column with the possessive pronouns, just like *his*. *Who's* is a contraction, or a shortened form of *who is*. If you don't know whether to use *whose* or *who's*, break apart the contraction; ask yourself whether or not the question is asking *who is*.

6. (Who's/Whose) driving the car?

7. (Who's / Whose) shiny new car is that?

Who Is It?

Who is it? is a tricky question when looking for the correct pronoun. Notice again that *who* is in the subject pronouns column. Therefore, when you answer the question *Who is it?* you must choose a subject pronoun.

8. When I answered the phone, a voice asked, "Who is it?" I had no choice but to reply, "It is _____."

Answers can be found on page 40.

ONE MORE THING...

Pronouns allow you to describe the same person or thing without being repetitive. Imagine what a sentence would be like without pronouns.

> *Fatima and Miguel decided to visit Fatima and Miguel's aunt, so Fatima and Miguel drove Fatima and Miguel's car out to the country where Fatima and Miguel's aunt lives.*

What a long and redundant sentence! Wouldn't it be easier to say,

> *Fatima and Miguel decided to visit their aunt, so they drove their car out to the country where their aunt lives.*

Thus, you can use pronouns to construct sentences that are concise and do not repeat themselves too much.

Participate

Activity 1: Pronouns for Nouns

Directions: Using the One More Thing... box from the previous page as a model, write three long sentences, each full of nouns and no pronouns. Then switch sentences with a partner. Rewrite your partner's sentences more concisely by replacing the nouns with pronouns. Answers will vary.

YOUR SENTENCES:

1.

2.

3.

YOUR PARTNER'S REWRITES:

1.

2.

3.

Activity 2: Hands-On

Go back through that magazine/newspaper page from the last lesson and pick a pronoun that could replace each noun you circled.

In a Nutshell

Skills

- A **personal pronoun** replaces a person or thing. It is less specific than the noun that it replaces, but it can do all the things nouns can do.

- An **interrogative pronoun** replaces a person or thing that is not known. It usually appears in a question.

- Two groups of **interrogative pronouns** that are often misused are *who* and *whom*, and *whose* and *who is*.

Answers for Explore:

1. Who
2. When
3. Where
4. him
5. whom
6. Who's
7. Whose
8. I

Noun and Pronoun Agreement

Nouns describe a person, place, or thing. **Pronouns** describe the same person, place, or thing. Pronouns are words that replace a noun so that you do not have to repeat the same noun over and over again.

At the end of this lesson, you will be able to:

- understand what pronouns do

- find pronouns and their antecedents in text

- figure out whether a pronoun agrees with its antecedent

- write sentences using pronouns in the right gender, number, and case

Parent's Corner

Fifth graders can easily mix up singular and plural agreement with pronouns. To solidify this lesson, while you are reading with your fifth grader, challenge them to pick out pronouns in the text and—importantly—identify which noun the pronoun is referring to in the sentence.

Dive Right In!

Pronoun Perfection

Directions: Summarize the plot of your favorite movie in ten sentences. Be sure to use pronouns and include at least two indefinite pronouns. Make sure your pronouns match their antecedents in number. Answers will vary.

Explore

Pronouns

As you learned in a previous lesson, a **pronoun** is a word that replaces a noun. Pronouns are useful in communication so that you do not have to repeat the same nouns. This creates more efficient communication. Look at the following example.

⇨ Maggie took *her* younger brother to the scary movie, and later that night *they* had nightmares.

Her is the pronoun that refers to *Maggie*; *they* is the pronoun that refers to *Maggie and her younger brother*. Think about how weird speaking and writing would be without pronouns! If we did not use pronouns, our sentences would be long and funny sounding, like this.

⇨ Maggie took Maggie's younger brother to the scary movie, and later that night Maggie and Maggie's younger brother had nightmares.

The Antecedent

Almost all pronouns refer to an **antecedent**. The antecedent is the noun that the pronoun replaces. In the previous sentence, *Maggie* is the antecedent for *her*, *Maggie and her younger brother* is the antecedent for *they*, and *her* is the antecedent for *Maggie's*. In the sentence that follows, circle the pronoun and underline the antecedent.

1. The gnome was so exhausted that he could not finish the hike up the long and winding mountainous trail.

Typically, but not always, the antecedent comes before the pronoun that replaces it. Sometimes, though, the pronoun can come first, and the antecedent follows it. In the sentence that follows, circle the pronoun and underline the antecedent.

2.   After eating her dinner of garlicky spinach, the girl felt strong and ready to combat evil.

Agreement

Mastering the use of pronouns and recognizing antecedents will help you through the majority of your encounters with pronouns. However, teachers and test-makers often judge the toughest part of pronouns: agreement. When writing, always check to make sure your pronouns agree with their antecedents in gender, number, and case.

Gender

Pronouns typically match their antecdents in **gender**. Gender refers to whether the antecedent is male, female, or neutral. Look at this example.

⇨   Kim loved to swim, so she went to the lake every weekend.

Kim is female, so the pronoun *she* replaces *Kim*. If we replaced *Kim* with *it*, the sentence would not make sense.

How would you replace the nouns in this sentence with pronouns?

3.   Jim won the marathon.

As we mentioned earlier in this chapter, "they" is a plural pronoun that can be used for a mix of male and female antecedents. For example: All of the neighborhood kids—George, Bianca, Shalewa, and Aaron--they all love ice cream.

Number

Number refers to whether the pronoun is singular or plural. A pronoun must agree in number with its antecedent: Singular pronouns replace singular antecedents, and plural pronouns replace plural antecedents.

What is wrong with this sentence? Circle the pronoun and underline the antecedent.

4.   The dogs in the pen have received its immunity and vitamin shots.

Do the pronoun and antecedent agree in number? No! *Dogs* is plural, but *it* is singular. What is the correct sentence?

Answers can be found on page 48.

ONE MORE THING...

To express yourself clearly, your pronouns must agree with their antecedents. Pronouns without clear antecedents make vague or ambiguous sentences. Imagine trying to understand a conversation with bad pronouns or missing antecedents.

Each has received their shots. The first girl is without his permission slip, but they eventually found them behind that. After receiving it, the first was tired and decided to sleep, instead of going to it.

To be understood and communicate effectively, always use matching pronouns and antecedents in your sentences. This skill is so important that you will see it judged on many standardized tests, by your teachers at school, and by future employers who require good communication abilities.

Participate

Activity: Hands-On

Think of your favorite book or TV show or video game. Go through the list of characters and write a list of the pronouns that could apply. For example, if your favorite favorite book/show is *The Babysitter's Club*, you could have:

Claudia	her, she, hers
Kristy	her, she, hers
Logan	he, him, his
The whole club	theirs, they

Now you try it.

In a Nutshell

Skills

- A pronoun replaces a noun to avoid repetition in a sentence. The noun that the pronoun replaces is called the **antecedent**.

- Pronouns must agree with their antecedents in number. A singular antecedent takes a singular pronoun, and a plural antecedent takes a plural pronoun.

Answers for Explore:

1. The pronoun is he; the antecedent is gnome (or the gnome).

2. The pronoun is her; the antecedent is girl (or the girl).

3. He won it. Explain that if you replace Jim and marathon with the wrong pronouns, the whole sentence changes meaning. She won him.

4. The pronoun is its, and the antecedent is dogs. The correct sentence is The dogs in the pen have received their immunity and vitamin shots.

Verbs

Every sentence contains a **verb**. The verb is what is happening in the sentence. It is a word that expresses an action or a state of being.

At the end of this lesson, you will be able to:

- understand what verbs do

- find verbs in text

- identify and use the correct tense of a verb

- write sentences using verbs correctly

Parent's Corner

Fifth graders use verbs all day long, but it's always important to make sure they actually *notice* that they are using verbs, not just in writing, but in speech as well. You might ask them to name 5 nouns and 5 verbs to check their understanding. Or look through a cookbook and ask them to point to all the verbs they say. Make sure to explain that verbs are action words—and they can be acted out, as well, for added fun!

Dive Right In!

Find the Verbs

Directions: Circle all the verbs in the passage below and determine whether they are past, present, or future tense:

Today was an eventful day. I awoke earlier than usual and decided to take advantage of the temperate weather. Since we are entering the peak of spring, the mornings here are warm and peaceful. I chose the park as the site of my morning yoga. (For the past few weeks, I have been going there occasionally.) I walked about 20 feet away from my house before I realized that I had foolishly forgotten my yoga mat. Just as I was about to turn back for home, I said to myself, "Let's try something new. I will do my yoga practice without a mat, on the grass!" Later, while I was washing the mud and dirt off of my hands and knees, I had the slightest tinge of regret. But, ultimately, the experience was fun—and I will do it again sometime!

Answers can be found on page 60.

Explore

Every Sentence Needs a Verb

To express a complete thought, every sentence you write needs a verb. Without a verb, the words are a **fragment**. What is happening in the following quotations?

"Jason."

"In the world of your daffodils."

"Dense village."

"With a tail, Angela."

"Presently, the pharmacist."

These "sentences" don't make any sense! They are fragments without verbs, so we don't know what is happening.

Action Verbs

An **action verb** expresses what someone or something is doing or what is happening. For example, *dance*, *talk*, and *drink* are all action verbs: They are all things you can do.

Identify and circle the action verb in this sentence.

1.   The star cast its light on the face of the planet.

This sentence is about *what the star is doing*: the star *is casting its light,* so *cast* is the action verb in the sentence.

Linking Verbs

A **linking verb**, also called a **state-of-being verb,** tells you that something is or exists. It often links the subject to information about the subject: The duck *is* in the room. This kind of verb doesn't express action; the duck isn't actually doing anything. Rather, the verb just tells us the duck's location. State-of-being verbs indicate the subject's condition, circumstance, or location.

Identify and circle the state-of-being verb in this sentence, and underline the information that is provided about the subject.

2. In my dream, I was at the center of a dark forest filled with flashing fireflies.

The narrator *was* at the center of the forest, so *was* is the verb expressing his state of being; the information about the narrator is that he was *at the center of a dark forest filled with flashing fireflies.*

Verb Tense

Not only do verbs indicate the actions or state of being of a subject, but they also give us a sense of *when* these actions or feelings are taking place. The **verb tense** used indicates whether something happened or is happening in the past, present, or future.

The **infinitive** is the most basic form of the verb. It is composed of the word *to* and the base verb: *to be, to bite, to think, to run, to seem, to play, to write, to sing,* and so on.

Present Tense

The present tense indicates that the action is happening now. The **simple present tense** is formed by removing the *to* from the infinitive and adding a subject before it. The infinitive verb *to wander* becomes *I wander, you wander,* and *they wander.* The exception is the *he, she,* and *it* pronouns, as well as any other singular noun. Add *–s* to the verb in these cases: *she wanders, he wanders,* and *the lonely cow wanders.*

Circle the simple present tense verbs in the following example.

3. A bass worm is a type of fishing lure with white spots. Bass respond to it better than to other plastic worms because it is shiny and smells like licorice.

Past Tense

Write with the past tense when the action has already happened. In general, to turn a verb into the **simple past tense**, add *–ed* to the end of the base verb.

Circle the past tense verbs in the next example.

4.   She traveled into the Amazon hoping to see exotic birds; however, she instead discovered the red fire ants when they quickly crawled up her legs.

Future Tense

Use verbs in the **simple future tense** to describe something that is going to happen sometime in the future but has not happened yet. In general, to turn a verb into the *simple future tense*, add *will* before the base verb. Note that the future tense does *not* take the final *–s* in the third person singular as does the simple present tense. For example, you say that *he will stop*, not *he will stops*.

Circle the simple future tense verbs in the following example.

5.   The sun will rise tomorrow. It will appear low in the east and will climb the horizon until high noon, when it will shine directly down on the Earth.

Timing

Sentences often have time indicators to show whether the sentence takes place in the present, past, or future. Words such as *now, at this time,* and *currently* suggest the present tense. *Yesterday, earlier, last week, years ago,* and *then* indicate the past tense. The future tense is often accompanied by words like *tomorrow, eventually,* and *next.* Using time words in conjunction with tense will help clarify your writing.

Let's Go Shopping

Here's a list of how a regular verb is conjugated in present, past, and future tenses. **Conjugated** means to change the form of the verb based on the subject and tense used.

Infinitive Verb: To Shop

Subject	Present Tense	Past Tense	Future Tense	Participle
I	shop	shopped	will shop	shopped
you	shop	shopped	will shop	shopped
he, she, it	shops	shopped	will shop	shopped
we	shop	shopped	will shop	shopped
you (plural)	shop	shopped	will shop	shopped
they	shop	shopped	will shop	shopped

Identify and circle the subject in the following sentences. Then use the time clues to fill in the correct conjugation of the verb *to shop*.

6. Every time she visits the mall, she _____ for shoes in her favorite stores.

7. Last week he _____ for the newest CD from his favorite musician so that he could be the first to have it.

8. Next week they _____ for her birthday present so that they will have it ready in time for the party.

Answers can be found on page 60.

Irregular Verbs

The basic rules for forming the tenses of verbs become tougher with certain verbs. These are called **irregular verbs** because they don't follow the normal conjugations into past, present, and future tense. Look at this sentence.

⇨ We *were* not long in learning the intention of our captors. They *were* determined to hold us until the storm passed. These captors *were* actually saving us from our foolish attempt to travel during the tornado.

The word *were* appears several times. *Were* is actually the plural past tense of the *to be* verb. Look at the chart to see how the verb *to be* is conjugated in the present and past tense. You can also see that the future tense is still *will + base verb*. This is true for all irregular verbs.

Irregular Verb: To Be

Subject	Present Tense	Past Tense	Future Tense	Participle
I	am	was	will be	been
you	are	were	will be	been
he, she, it	is	was	will be	been
we	are	were	will be	been
you (plural)	are	were	will be	been
they	are	were	will be	been

ONE MORE THING... We need verbs to tell what is happening or in what state the subject is. Also, when we communicate, we need to let other people know at what time or in what sequence things occur. Try telling a story about what happened in the past while using verbs in the future tense. Or ask someone to do something now, but use the past tense! To be understood and communicate effectively, always use verbs in the appropriate tense in your sentences.

Participate

Activity 1: Verbalizing Your Activities

Directions: Think of an activity that you like to do or would like to try. Come up with ten verbs that can be used to describe or explain how you do that activity, and list the present, past, and future conjugations for that verb. Then, create ten sentences using those verbs. Make sure that some sentences are in the past describing what you did, some are in the present describing what you are doing now, and some are in the future describing how you will continue that activity. Challenge yourself by using at least three irregular verbs! Answers will vary.

Activity:

Ten verbs:

1. Present, past, or future verb tenses:

   Your Sentence:

2. Present, past, or future verb tenses:

   Your Sentence:

3. Present, past, or future verb tenses:

   Your Sentence:

4. Present, past, or future verb tenses:

   Your Sentence:

5. Present, past, or future verb tenses:

   Your Sentence:

6. Present, past, or future verb tenses:

   Your Sentence:

7. Present, past, or future verb tenses:

   Your Sentence:

8. Present, past, or future verb tenses:

   Your Sentence:

9. Present, past, or future verb tenses:

   Your Sentence:

10. Present, past, or future verb tenses:

    Your Sentence:

Activity 2: Hands-On

Get up from your work and start verb-ing! As you do an action, say what action you are doing. See how long you can go. So, for example, you might start dancing (and aloud, say "dancing") then jumping then running then snapping then clapping.

In a Nutshell

Skills

- The **verb** in the sentence is the action in the sentence; the verb tells you what is happening.

- The tense of the verb (**past, present,** or **future**) tells you when the action happens.

- An **action verb** describes what someone or something is doing, whereas **linking verbs** tells us that something is or exists and in what state it exists.

Answers for Dive Right In:

Today **was (past)** an eventful day. I **awoke (past)** earlier than usual and **decided (past)** to take advantage of the temperate weather. Since we **are entering (present)** the peak of spring, the mornings here **are (present)** warm and peaceful. I **chose (past)** the park as the site of my morning yoga. (For the past few weeks, I **have been (past)** going there occasionally.) I **walked (past)** about 20 feet away from my house before I **realized (past)** that I **had (past)** foolishly **forgotten (past)** my yoga mat. Just as I **was (past)** about to turn back for home, I **said (past)** to myself, "**Let's (present)** try something new. I **will do (future)** my yoga practice without a mat, on the grass!" Later, while I **was washing (past)** the mud and dirt off of my hands and knees, I **had (past)** the slightest tinge of regret. But, ultimately, the experience **was (past)** fun—and I **will do (future)** it again sometime!

 Answers for Explore:

3. is, respond, is, smells
4. traveled, discovered, crawled
5. will rise, will appear, will climb, will shine
6. shops
7. shopped
8. will shop

Subject and Verb Agreement

Every sentence must have a subject and a verb. Additionally, the subject and the verb must agree with each other in number. A plural subject needs a plural verb, and a singular subject requires a singular verb.

At the end of this lesson, you will be able to:

- identify singular and plural subjects

- identify singular and plural verbs

- work with tricky or complex subjects

- make sure the subject and verb of a sentence agree

Parent's Corner

Don't be afraid to correct your fifth grader whenever they make a subject & verb agreement mistake. Ask them to summarize their day to you, either verbally or in writing. Make sure the subjects and verbs agree.

Dive Right In!

Verb in the Blank

Directions: Read the following sentences. Underline the subjects. Circle the correct verb to go in the blank.

1. A large part of the town's population _____ (is / are) running in the marathon.

2. A small group of townspeople _____ (was / were) watching the race.

3. Half of the town _____ (is / are) against the building of the new library.

4. The other citizens _____ (is / are) for the new library.

5. Wanda, together with her teammates, _____ (presents / present) a formidable opponent on the soccer field.

6. She seems to forget, however, that there _____ (are / is) other things to be done before she can earn a passing grade in English class.

7. The rain storms that drench this town every spring _____ (are / is) more than just a bothersome occurrence.

8. Most of the milk _____ (appear / appears) to be spoiled.

9. Some of the votes for class president _____ (seem / seems) to have been miscounted.

10. Either the teachers in this school or the principal _____ (is / are) going to have to make a decision about the vote.

Answers can be found on page 70.

Explore

Singular & Plural Subjects

The **subject** of a sentence tells who or what the sentence is about. Plural subjects refer to multiple persons, places, things, or ideas. Singular subjects only reference one person, place, thing, or idea.

Circle the subject in the sentence that follows. Is it singular or plural?

1.   The stone hit the walrus on the end of his nose.

Now try this sentence.

2.   The other walruses rolled with laughter on the beach.

Singular & Plural Verbs

Verbs express actions and states of being. The verb form in a sentence must match the form of the subject. If the subject is singular, the verb must be singular. If the verb is plural, the subject must be plural.

Circle the correct verb form in the following sentence.

3.   The walrus (use / uses) its tusks to pull itself out of the water, to break holes in the ice, and to fight.

In this sentence, the subject—*walrus*—is singular, so the verb must also be singular.

Which verb form is correct in this sentence?

4. Walruses sometimes (kills / kill) polar bears.

Here, the subject is *walruses*, which is plural. Use the plural form of the verb.

Tricky Subjects

Making subjects and verbs agree can be complicated. Sometimes it is hard to figure out whether a subject is singular or plural. Here are a few rules to help.

Rule #1: Some pronouns are singular subjects. Here is a list.

anybody	anyone	anything	anywhere	each	one
everybody	everyone	everything	everywhere	much	less
somebody	someone	something	somewhere	either	little
nobody	no one	nothing	nowhere	neither	

Underline the singular pronoun in the following sentence. Circle the verb that agrees.

5. Each of the boys (is / are) planning a different Saturday activity.

Rule #2: Other pronouns are plural subjects. Here is a list.

both	several	few	fewer	many

Underline the plural pronoun in the following sentence, and circle the correct verb.

6. Several of the flowers (is / are) pink, while the others are a light purple color.

Rule #3: Some pronouns can be either singular or plural subjects depending on the context.

all	some	any	enough
most	more	none	

Underline the pronouns in the following sentences, and then write whether they are used as singular or plural pronouns. Circle the verb that agrees with the subject in number.

7.   All of the peanut butter chocolate chip cookies (is / are) gone.

8.   By the end of the day, all of the energy (was / were) gone from the once lively students.

Rule #4: Two or more singular subjects joined by the word *and* always make a **compound subject**, or a plural subject.

Underline the subject in the sentence. Then circle the correct verb.

9.   Asia and Cory (like / likes) to explore mysterious places in hopes of proving mythical creatures exist.

Asia and Cory together make a plural subject because there are two people.

Rule #5: When using the phrases *either/or* and *neither/nor,* the verb must agree with the last subject in the phrase.

Underline the last subject in the sentence. Then circle the correct verb.

10.   Neither the scientists nor the geologist (know / knows) the thickness of the Earth's crust, despite all their equipment to measure it.

Rule #6: Collective nouns refer to groups of things, but they are singular. Some examples of collective nouns include a jury, government, class, or group.

Underline the collective noun. Then circle the correct verb.

11. The team of zoologists (is / are) looking for a solution to the panda bear problem.

Answers can be found on page 70.

ONE MORE THING... If your subjects and verbs agree, you will be able to communicate effectively. Effective communication is important when you are interviewing for a job or when you are trying to persuade someone to agree with you. When you write and speak more formally in school, it is easier to earn good grades since writing and speaking are important skills in all subjects. Sometimes, all it takes to impress people is great grammar!

Participate

Activity: Hands-On

With a friend or sibling, work on subject and verb agreement. You can start by saying a subject (who or what the sentence is about) then your friend can create the rest of the sentence using an agreeing verb.

For example, you say: the kittens. Then your partner could create a sentence and say, "are hungry" and "are" is plural so it agrees with plural kittens. Go back and forth like this with different subjects, then verb/rest of sentence creation.

In a Nutshell

Skills

- The **subject** of a sentence tells who or what the sentence is about.

- **Plural subjects** refer to multiple persons, places, things, or ideas. **Singular subjects** only reference one person, place, thing, or idea.

- **Verbs** express actions and states of being. The verb form in a sentence must match the form of the subject. If the subject is singular, the verb must be singular. if the verb is plural, the subject must be plural.

Answers for Dive Right In:

1. is
2. was
3. is
4. are
5. presents
6. are
7. are
8. appears
9. seem
10. is

 Answers for Explore:

1. The subject of this sentence is *the stone*. Since there is only one stone mentioned, it is a singular subject.

2. In this sentence, the subject is *the other walruses*. There is more than one walrus, so the subject is plural.

3. uses

4. kill

5. is (*Each* is singular, therefore it matches up with *is planning*.)

6. Plural pronoun: several
   Verb: are
   (*Several* is plural; therefore, it matches up with *are*.)

7. Pronoun: all (plural)
   Verb: are
   (*All* refers to the *cookies*, a plural noun. Therefore, the correct verb is *are*.)

8. Pronoun: all (singular)
   Verb: was
   (*All* refers to *energy*, which is a singular noun. Now the correct verb is *was*.)

9. Subject: Asia and Cory
   Verb: like
   (The correct verb is *like*, as in *they like*.)

10. Last Subject: geologist
    Verb: knows
    (The last subject is *geologist*, which is singular, so the correct verb form is *knows*.)

11. Collective Noun: team
    Verb: is
    (Even though there may be many zoologists on the *team*, the team itself is singular. *Team* is a collective noun because it treats all of the members of the team as one unit. The correct verb is *is*.)

Adjectives and Adverbs

Adjectives and adverbs are the description words in sentences. **Adjectives** describe nouns and pronouns. **Adverbs** describe verbs, adjectives, and other adverbs.

At the end of this lesson, you will be able to:

- understand what adjectives and adverbs do

- find adjectives and adverbs in text

- differentiate between adverbs and adjectives

- write sentences using adjectives and adverbs correctly

Parent's Corner

Adjectives and adverbs can be fun ways to add details and specificity into writing. How can you encourage your student to be more specific? When the student notices a dog on the street, challenge them to be more specific when they describe the animal. What kind of dog? Big, small? What color? Does it have an attitude? Friendly, tired? Challenge your student to describe *how* the animal moves, too. How many *-ly* adverbs can you come up with as a family? (gracefully, clumsily, proudly, amiably, etc.)

Dive Right In!

Favorite Food

Directions: Write a paragraph about your favorite food. Do not use any adjectives or adverbs. Answers will vary.

Paragraph WITHOUT adjectives or adverbs

Now, write the same paragraph WITH adjectives and adverbs

Explore

Adjectives

Adjectives answer the following questions about nouns and pronouns:

> What kind?
>
> Which one?
>
> How much?
>
> How many?

Circle the adjective in this sentence.

1.   When you visit Kenya, try not to meet an angry hippopotamus.

Angry answers the question "What kind of hippopotamus?" Therefore, *angry* is an adjective that describes a hippopotamus.

Often, but not always, the adjective comes before the noun. If we change the sentence to read "The hippopotamus is angry," *angry* is still the adjective, and it still describes the hippopotamus.

Other Adjectives

Adjectives also answer the question "Which one?" Some of these adjectives are called **articles**, and some are called **demonstratives**. Articles describe members of a group. Demonstratives, however, are more specific; they describe particular nouns in terms of where they are.

Articles	Demonstratives
a	this
an	that
the	these
	those

Consider the following sentences.

⇨ "*The* shirt is black."

This sentence describes a specific shirt by using the word *the*, but we do not know anything about where the shirt is.

⇨ *This* shirt is my favorite because it is red and fits perfectly.

This shirt tells us that the author is talking about the shirt nearby. *This* shirt is closer to the speaker than all the other shirts. If the shirt is not the closest, the speaker can show its nearness by pointing to it.

⇨ *That* shirt is dirty and needs to be washed.

That shirt tells us that the shirt the author describes is *over there*, which is a good thing if it is dirty and smelly!

Adverbs

Adverbs answer the following questions about verbs, adjectives, and other adverbs:

> How?
>
> Where?
>
> When?
>
> How often?
>
> How much?

Write the questions these italicized adverbs answer underneath each sentence.

2.   The parakeet flew *quickly* back to its cage.

3.   He arrives *early* to work every Monday.

4.   Melissa showed off her *very* polished trophy.

Answers can be found on page 80.

Many, but not all, adverbs end in *-ly*. Some notable exceptions intensify meaning or describe places and time. Additionally, not all words that end in *-ly* are adverbs. For instance, *jolly, gnarly,* and *silly* are adjectives because they describe nouns. To differentiate adjectives and adverbs, rely on the word's purpose rather than its spelling!

Adverbs that Don't Use *-ly*

Intensifiers	Place Words	Time Words
very	outside	today
quite	inside	tomorrow
rather	there	yesterday
too	here	always
well	everywhere	never

ONE MORE THING... Adjective and adverbs allow writers to describe places and situations. Sentences without adjectives and adverbs are nearly naked! Consider the following sentences which lack any descriptive words:

I sang at concert.

Movie scares me.

Let's spice up those sentences! Check out these revised versions and witness the power of adjectives and adverbs.

I sang horribly at the school concert last night, though everyone, including myself, thought it was incredibly funny.

That famous movie about the crazy clowns still scares me today.

By including adjectives and adverbs in our sentences, we are able to create a more vivid picture of what's happening for the reader or listener.

Participate

Activity 1: Boring Sentences

Directions: Enhance these boring sentences with adjectives and adverbs. Answers will vary.

1. Comedians use humor.

2. Sugar ruins teeth.

3. He wore hats.

4. Songs are censored.

5. Seals play.

Activity 2: Hands-On

On one side of an index card, write a very "naked" sentence that doesn't have much to it (like the "One More Thing..." exercise on page 76). On the other side of the card, write a better version of that sentence with tons of adjectives and adverbs. Speak these sentences out loud to an adult, saying the "naked" sentences very quietly and performing the improved, exciting sentences nice and loud.

In a Nutshell

Skills

- **Adjectives** answer the following questions about nouns and pronouns: What kind? Which one? How much? How many?

- **Articles** and **demonstratives** are the two kinds of adjectives that answer the question, "Which one?"

- **Adverbs** describe verbs, adjectives, and other adverbs. Adverbs answer the following questions about verbs, adjectives, and other adverbs: How? Where? When? How often? How much?

Answers for Explore:

2. How did it fly?

3. When did he arrive?

4. How was it polished? Very. Notice that *very* modifies an adjective.

Finding the Main Idea and Supporting Evidence

When you skim a passage, you've already done most of the work to find the main idea. The **main idea** of any passage is what the author is trying to tell you or persuade you to believe. You also need to go deeper into the passage to determine what the **supporting evidence** is.

At the end of this lesson, you will be able to:

- use skills you have to help find the main idea

- refine your understanding of how to find the main idea

- use skills you have to help find the supporting evidence

Parent's Corner

Fifth graders, when you ask them to tell you the main idea of a chapter or an entire book, will often launch into a long-winded summary ("first there was a girl named Sarah and she lived in a cottage. She was living a very nice life but then a storm came…"). It can be hard for them to identify the *main* point of a piece of text, to synthesize everything into one clear idea. After you read a chapter of a book with your student, ask them what the three most important details are, and, if possible, distill it down to *one* main idea.

Dive Right In!

Uncovering the Main Idea

Directions: Read the following passage. Translate any difficult words. Underline all of the sentences and words that make up the main idea. Cross off the extra details that aren't included in the main idea.

Whistle While You Work

When you want to talk to friends who live far away, you probably pick up the phone and call them. In some places where telephones are not as common, people use a language of whistles to talk to one another. The island of La Gomera, part of the Canary Islands off the coast of Spain, has a language like this. The island has many mountains, and the villages are so distant that it would take too long to travel from one village to another to talk to friends. So people on the island have learned a language of whistles.

When people on La Gomera need to talk to someone in the next village, they whistle. They whistle so loudly that the sound can be heard up to five miles away. And it's not just one simple sound; it's a complex language that people use to talk about many things. The villagers can talk about the weather and other topics that have an effect on their lives. The whistle language sounds like music and is usually very important communication.

1. What is the topic of the passage?

2. What is the most important thing the author says about the topic?

3. Do the other sentences in the passage either lead up to or support this idea?

4. List the supporting details for the main idea.

Answers can be found on page 90.

# **Explore**

How to Find the Main Idea

Finding the main idea is an essential step to understanding the text you're reading. When you are skimming to find the main idea, look for answers to the following questions:

1.   What is the topic of the passage?

2.   What is the most important thing the author says about the topic?

3.   Do the other sentences in the passage either lead up to or support this idea?

Let's try an example. Skim this passage from the health book *Physiology and Hygiene for Secondary Schools*, by Francis M. Walters. You'll notice some words in **bold** throughout this passage. Those are words that you may wish to look up in a dictionary, if you don't know them. After you read and look up as needed, answer the questions that follow.

⇨   Disease, which is some **upset** of the vital functions, may be due to a variety of causes. Some of these causes, such as **hereditary** defects, are remote and beyond the control of the individual. Others are the result of negligence in the observance of well-recognized hygienic rules. Others still are of the nature of influences, such as climate, the house in which one lives, or one's method of gaining a livelihood, that produce changes in the body— **imperceptible** at the time, but, in the long run, laying the foundations of disease. And last, and strongest, are the **minute** living organisms, called germs, that find their way into the body.

1. What is the topic of the passage?

2. What is the most important thing the author says about the topic?

3. Do the other sentences in the passage either lead up to or support this idea?

Once you are skilled at finding the main idea, the difficulty of a text no longer matters. It may take a little longer to get through the passage because, instead of skimming, you may need to read and translate.

Let's attempt a harder example. Skim the following introduction to *The Notebooks of Leonardo da Vinci*. As you skim, underline the words and sentences that make up the main idea. Cross out any information that isn't relevant to the main point. Write notes about the main idea in the margin. Then answer the three questions that follow.

⇨ Among all the studies of natural causes, Light chiefly delights the beholder; and among the great features of Mathematics, the way it affects our vision is what attracts the mind of the investigator. Perspective, therefore, must be preferred to all the **discourses** and systems of human learning. Perspective, as it influences drawing, is divided into three principal sections. To paint accurately, the subjects of a painting should appear in **relief**. The grounds surrounding them at different distances shall properly sit within the picture by means of the 3 branches of Perspective: the reduction in the **distinctness** of the forms of the objects, the shrinking in their magnitude, and the lessening of their color.

4. What is the topic of the passage?

5. What is the most important thing the author says about the topic?

6. Do the other sentences in the passage either lead up to or support this idea?

If you are not quite sure what the main idea is, read through the text very carefully. As you read each sentence, ask yourself if it supports or weakens what you think is the main idea. Put a plus sign (+) for strengthening or a minus sign (−) for weakening over each one. When you reach the end of the passage, count your pluses and minuses. If you have more pluses, you found the main idea. If you have more minuses, try to redefine your main idea and start over.

Next, reread the passage more carefully in search of support for your main idea. Underline the **supporting evidence** in the passage. Then answer the questions that follow.

⇨ Among all the studies of natural causes, Light chiefly delights the beholder; and among the great features of Mathematics, the way it affects our vision is what attracts the mind of the investigator. Perspective, therefore, must be preferred to all the **discourses** and systems of human learning. Perspective, as it influences drawing, is divided into three principal sections. To paint accurately, the subjects of a painting should appear in **relief**. The grounds surrounding them at different distances shall properly sit within the picture by means of the 3 branches of Perspective: the reduction in the **distinctness** of the forms of the objects, the shrinking in their magnitude, and the lessening of their color.

7. Which supporting details are strongest? Place a star (*) above them in the text.

8. Are there any details that contradict the main idea? Place a minus sign (−) above them in the text.

Answers can be found on page 90.

Using Support

Once you know how to find supporting evidence, you can use it to answer reading comprehension questions on tests, to write essays about texts, and to enjoy literature more thoroughly.

Look again at the parts of the passage that you underlined. Translate just those parts into your own words. In the space below, write down, in your own words, the main idea followed by the important details.

1. Is your version as convincing as the original? Why or why not?

2. What advantages does your version have over the original?

3. How could this version help you in school?

Have you ever read something and, when you finished, realized that you had no idea what you just read? Knowing the main idea of the reading helps focus your efforts. By reading purposefully, you approach the text in a different way. Instead of passively allowing words to march across your line of vision, you are choosing actively what is important and what to remember based on the main idea.

When you assert a strong opinion, others may ask you to back up your view with facts. Understanding how to find and use supporting evidence is essential to successfully proving your point. Think about election season. How do politicians convince people to vote for them? They describe what they stand for and then they support their stance with a list of achievements they have accomplished for their cause. When people vote, they select the politician whose supporting evidence best matches their own views.

Participate

Activity 1: Hands-On

Find 3 articles in a magazine, newspaper, or website. Read each article thoroughly then summarize the main idea out loud.

Activity 2: Hands-On

Using the same 3 articles from before, underline or highlight the examples within the article that support the main idea of each article.

In a Nutshell

Skills

When you are skimming to find the **main idea**, look for answers to the following questions:

1. What is the topic of the passage?
2. What is the most important thing the author says about the topic?
3. Do the other sentences in the passage either lead up to or support this idea?

- For a main idea to exist, it must have **supporting evidence** in the text.

- Once you know how to find supporting evidence, you can use it to answer reading comprehension questions on tests, to write essays about texts, and to enjoy literature more thoroughly.

Answers for Dive Right In:

1. Topic: the language of whistles on the island of La Gomera

2. The whistle language isn't simple; it's a complex way people communicate various ideas.

3. Yes, the other sentences support this idea.

4. Supporting details: the whistling can be heard up to 5 miles away; islanders use whistling to convey many different topics, such as the weather.

 Answers for Explore:

How to Find the Main Idea

1. Disease and its various causes

2. Disease may have many causes.

3. Yes, the other sentences support the idea.

4. Perspective in art

5. Perspective and its 3 branches are the most important things to learn.

6. Yes, the other sentences support the idea.

7. Supporting details that are strong (*): "3 branches of perspective: the reduction in the distinctness of the forms of the objects, the shrinking in their magnitude, and the lessening of their color."

8. There are no details here that contradict the main idea (-).

Rereading

After reading a long passage, whether it is informational or narrative, you may find it difficult to remember all of the information it contained. To work with the passage, you may have to go back to the text for specific information. This is called **rereading.**

At the end of this lesson, you will be able to:

- understand when to reread

- understand how to reread

Parent's Corner

Reading texts closely for details is an important skill in fifth grade. On first glance, your student may think she knows exactly what she's read, but may have missed important aspects of the text. Consider writing the text "Paris in the the spring" on a piece of paper (notice the *two* "the"s!) and asking your fifth grader to read it aloud. Many fifth graders will read it as "Paris in the spring." Show them how they may be moving too quickly through texts and need to slow down. Additionally, after each paragraph or chapter in a book, if your student cannot explain to you what has happened in the story, encourage the student to go back and reread. There is no shame in this! Just slow down and read every word carefully to catch all the rich details of a story.

Dive Right In!

Reread for More

Directions: Follow these directions in order as you read the passage on the following page.

1.   Skim.

   a.   What is the topic?

   b.   What is the main idea?

2.   Read the questions on the next page and determine the following:

   a.   Will you scan or reread to answer question 1? Why?

   b.   Will you scan or reread to answer question 2? Why?

   c.   Will you scan or reread to answer question 3? Why?

3.   Read the passage.

4.   Find and record the answers to the questions.

Manners, Custom and Dress During the Middle Ages and During the Renaissance Period

Paul Lacroix

The great movement for the creation of the **bourgeoisie** dates from the eleventh to the thirteenth centuries. Simultaneously we see the bourgeois appear, already rich and luxurious, parading on all occasions their personal wealth. Their private life could only be an imitation of that in the wealthier nobles. By degrees, wealth strengthened and improved their condition, and rendered them independent. They tried to **procure** luxuries equal or analogous to those enjoyed by the upper classes, which appeared to them the height of material happiness. In all times, the small have imitated the great. It was in vain that the upper classes threatened to crush this tendency to equality, which alarmed them. They unsuccessfully issued edicts, laws, regulations, and ordinances. However, the arbitrary restrictions which the nobility laid upon the lower classes gradually disappeared, and the power of wealth displayed itself in spite of all their efforts to suppress it.

Down to the thirteenth century, however rich their fathers or husbands might be, the women of the bourgeoisie were not permitted, without incurring a fine, to wear the clothing and ornaments exclusively reserved for the nobility. However, the monarchs frequently honored the bourgeoisie with government posts and treasures instead of enforcing the laws to separate the classes. Thus, the whole bourgeoisie gloried in the marks of distinction given to their representatives, and the ladies of this class, proud of their immense fortunes, but above all proud of the **municipal** powers held by their families, decorated themselves, regardless of expense, with costly furs and rich stuffs, despite the fact that they were forbidden by law to do so.

Reading Comprehension Questions

1. Who were the bourgeoisie imitating in "their private life"?

    a. Scan or reread?

    b. Why?

    c. Answer:

2. What type of rules did the nobility impose on the bourgeoisie?

    a. Scan or reread?

    b. Why?

    c. Answer:

3. How did kings show respect for the bourgeoisie?

    a. Scan or reread?

    b. Why?

    c. Answer:

Answers can be found on page 100.

Explore

When to Reread

Use **rereading** to understand a text fully, to write an essay with detailed supporting evidence, and to answer certain reading comprehension questions. We're going to focus on answering reading comprehension questions in this chapter. Essentially, you reread text when a question asks you for information you cannot scan for directly. It requires you to examine a part of the text in-depth instead of scanning for a word or phrase.

Because scanning is more straightforward, students usually prefer it as a way to find answers to reading comprehension questions. However, sometimes you can't find the word you're scanning for, and an obvious synonym doesn't pop out of the text. That's when you need to reread.

How to Reread

When you choose to reread a text, there is a reason. You are looking for something specific. Define that something in words. Imagine, for example, that you have a grocery list with the following items on it:

- bread
- milk
- oranges
- paper towels
- eggs
- potatoes

Mysteriously, your grocery list has reading comprehension questions at the bottom. The first question asks, "Are you going to buy eggs?" How would you answer it? You would glance at the list and quickly **scan** it for the word *eggs*. In this instance, you use scanning because you are looking for an exact word.

Sometimes, the answers to questions aren't as obvious. The next question on your grocery list asks, "What fruit are you going to purchase?"

How would you tackle this one? Would you look for the word *fruit* like you looked for the word *eggs*? Probably not. Few people create grocery lists in such general terms as *fruit*. Instead, you would examine the text for *specific* fruit. Words like *bananas, apples,* and *strawberries* might be possibilities. Your brain organizes words into groups, and you are searching for a word that fits into the group of *fruit*. Unlike scanning, rereading is slower. It requires reading thoughtfully and analytically.

When you start to re-examine a text, ask yourself the following questions to focus your efforts:

1. What word or phrase am I looking for?
2. Am I looking for a specific word or phrase or its synonym? Then scan.
3. Am I looking for a group of possible words or phrases? Then reread.

Apply these questions to the following excerpt from Edgar Allan Poe's poem "The Raven."

⇨ Open here I flung the shutter, when, with many a flirt and flutter,
In there stepped a stately Raven of the saintly days of yore.
Not the least obeisance made he; not an instant stopped or stayed he;
But, with mien of lord and lady, perched above my chamber door—
Perched upon a bust of Pallas just above my chamber door—
Perched and sat and nothing more.

Reading Comprehension Question: What bird enters the narrator's window?

1. What word or phrase am I looking for?

2. Am I looking for a specific word or phrase or its synonym? Then scan.

3. Am I looking for a group of possible words or phrases? Then reread.

What's the answer?

Answers can be found on page 100.

ONE MORE THING... Rereading is a great way to gather little details from a text to understand it fully, to answer reading comprehension questions, and to write essays full of supporting evidence. However, wouldn't it be wonderful if you read a passage so thoroughly that you didn't need to reread it?

Even the best readers' eyes get tired and their attention wanders. One way to make the most of your time is to read with a pen in hand. At the end of each sentence, mentally ask yourself, "Did I understand that?" If you answer no, put a check mark next to it and move on to the next one. At the end of your reading, return to the sentences with check marks and try to translate them. Ask for help if you need it. Although being so conscious of how you read means you will have to read more slowly, you will minimize your need to reread!

Participate

Activity: Hands-On

Pull out a book that you have ready before and reread the first page. Knowing what you know about how the story unfolds, think about that first page and how it sets the scene. Think about the way that rereading that first page feels, knowing that you have already read the entire book before.

In a Nutshell

Skills

- **Rereading** requires you to look at a particular part of the text in depth instead of scanning for a word or phrase.

- Use rereading to answer difficult questions or better understand a part of the passage.

Answers for Dive Right In:

1. a. Scan

   b. There is a quoted phrase you can hunt for in the text.

   c. Nobles

2. a. Reread

   b. "Type of rules" suggests a grouping question, like with fruit and bird earlier in the chapter.

   c. "Edicts, laws, regulations, and ordinances" or rules against bourgeoisie women dressing like the noble women

3. a. Scan or reread

   b. If students choose to scan, they can look for "show respect" and "kings." If students choose to reread, they can search for a grouping of respectful action by monarchs. Students' first inclination is to scan because it is easier and requires less complex thought. However, if the word or an obvious synonym doesn't pop out of the text, then they have to reread.

   c. They gave government posts and treasure.

 Answers for Explore:

What bird enters the narrator's window?

1. Searching for "bird."

2. I'm looking for a specific word, because the word "bird" is unlikely to appear on its own, since it's a gerneral term

3. I'm looking for a word that fits into the group "birds."

What's the answer? A raven

Essay Formats

To write a great essay, you need to understand its components and the different forms it can take. Knowing how to respond to assignments will help you best organize your writing.

At the end of this lesson, you will be able to:

- understand the different parts of an essay

- understand different types of essay prompts

- determine what writing style different prompts require

- gather the appropriate information to write different types of essays

Parent's Corner

At this age it is important for fifth graders to understand all the different ways you can express ideas. In your habitual reading with your student, try to vary the types of writing you share: make sure that you show your student nonfiction in addition to fiction. Also try to show students different examples of the sorts of essays they will be tasked with writing in school: newspaper op-eds are a great place to start looking. Ask your student what makes an effective or compelling argument? How do op-ed writers organize their essays? Does it work?

Dive Right In!

Activity: Before Writing

Directions: Read the sample assignments below and answer the questions.

Essay Prompt #1: The way that people perceive themselves is often different from the way that others perceive them. How do these differences in perception change people's lives?

1.   What type of essay is this? Why?

2.   Describe the information you would put in the essay.

Essay Prompt #2: Write a letter to the school newspaper demanding a shorter school day, which would give students time to have jobs, do homework, enjoy extracurricular activities, and spend time with their families.

1.   What type of essay is this? Why?

2.   Describe the information you would put in the essay.

Essay Prompt #3: Write a travel essay about the most popular tourist sites in your favorite country.

1. What type of essay is this? Why?

2. Describe the information you would put in the essay.

Essay Prompt #4: Examine the forces that led America to claim its independence from England.

1. What type of essay is this?

2. Describe the information you would put in the essay.

Answers can be found on page 110.

 **Explore**

Parts of an Essay

Each paragraph in an essay has a specific function. A paragraph can introduce your main idea, support your main idea, or wrap up the whole essay.

Introduction

Appearing at the beginning of your essay, the introduction begins to broadly address your topic. It presents your point and briefly highlights the examples you will use to support it. Finally, the introduction leads gracefully into your first body paragraph.

Body Paragraphs

Body paragraphs address the examples, in the order listed in the introduction, that demonstrate your point. These paragraphs support the examples with facts and details, and they explain how the examples directly and clearly support your idea. Sometimes, a body paragraph may address or disprove an argument that runs against your main idea.

Conclusion

The conclusion is your place to shine. It is where you get to show your ability to synthesize and comment on information. Use the conclusion to analyze the examples presented as a whole and to connect them to your main idea.

Types of Essay Assignments for Class

How would your teacher respond if you turned in a five-line poem when he had requested a ten-page research paper? When you sit down to write an essay, it is important to understand the assignment fully so you don't waste your time writing the wrong thing. Not all essay assignments require the same kind of writing. There are some basic categories that describe most essay prompts.

The Descriptive Assignment

The descriptive assignment asks you to describe something. Your goal is to inform the reader. A book report, a memoir, and a bird watching guide are all examples.

The Research Paper

A research paper, also known as a term paper, requires several trips to the library. One can be descriptive or argumentative. When writing a research paper, your goal is to examine a topic exhaustively, which may require you reading many different perspectives and authorities on that topic. For example, if you were researching the Renaissance, you would compile resources describing renaissance art, culture, politics, people, and places. Some teachers also ask you to form your own perspective based on all the information you've gathered, which also is part of many research papers.

The Argumentative Assignment

In an argumentative assignment, you explore all the facts of a topic, analyze them, and then form an opinion. This opinion is called a **thesis statement**. You write your paper with the intention of proving your thesis statement. You may need to research the topic so that you can support your view with facts. For example, if you are writing a paper about whether trans-fatty acids should be illegalized, you would research all the advantages and disadvantages of trans-fatty acids, study why they haven't been made illegal, and then propose, based on your facts, to ban them or not. What are two possible thesis statements you could have for this paper?

1.

2.

The Critical Assignment

A critical assignment is the most opinionated of all essays because it asks you to examine a topic and then judge it. Book reviews, literary criticism, movie reviews, and letters to the editor are all examples.

The Extreme Statement Assignment

Extreme statement assignments use extreme language. For example, "Do you agree or disagree with the following statement: Nothing is certain except death and taxes?" Words like always, never, all, none, and other words that indicate a finite extreme make it easy to disagree. Most people can think of at least *one* exception to a rule. Isn't change certain? If you claim to be watching everyone's favorite orangutan at the zoo, it would only take one person saying, "Hey, that's not my favorite orangutan!" to prove you wrong. If you decide to agree with an extreme statement, use indisputable facts for your supporting evidence. Someone who has been alive for 35 years was definitely born at some point. A plant that is now decomposing in its pot is certain not to grow bigger. You get the idea.

Room for Exceptions Assignment

Room for exceptions assignments make it easy to agree. All you have to do is say, "Yeah, sometimes this is true." To support your argument, just provide a few examples of truth. This is the easiest prompt in which to use conflicting examples. It practically begs you to do it: "It is sometimes true that cats get along with dogs. For example, my cat, Carrot, absolutely adored our golden retriever, Bones….However, it is not always true that cats get along with dogs. In a recent local newspaper story, a dog was drowned while trying to attack a cat on a boat. The article said that the cat appeared to be taunting the dog…"

Open-ended Assignment

Open-ended assignments require you to come up with a point of view all on your own (there is no "agree or disagree" involved) and support your view with relevant examples. For example, "Do you think men and women can remain friends after dating?" Another example is an essay that asks you to compare and contrast two ideas before selecting one: "Is it better to be loved or feared?"

ONE MORE THING...

Solid writing evolves from careful planning. The more you understand what an essay topic requires of you, the clearer and more appropriate your essay will be. Good writers never forget their goals. Businesses often ask to see a writing sample during the interview process to see how clearly and concisely you write. Employers often weigh a cover letter more than a resume when reviewing applications. How you write says a lot about how you think.

Participate

Activity: Hands-On

Knowing what you now know about essay formats, read an essay or article (online, in a newspaper or magazine) and note the Introduction, Body Paragraphs, and Conclusion. If you can, circle each part and write what it is in the margin.

In a Nutshell

Skills

- Each paragraph in an essay has a specific function. A paragraph can introduce your main idea, support your main idea, or wrap up the whole essay.

- When you sit down to write an essay, it is important to understand the assignment fully so you don't waste your time writing the wrong thing. Not all essay assignments require the same kind of writing. There are some basic categories that cover most essay assignments: Descriptive Essay, Research Paper, Argumentative Essay, Critical Essay, and Standardized Test Essay.

Answers for Dive Right In:

Essay Prompt #1

1. Open-ended. "How" tells us to create our own point of view; it doesn't ask us to agree or disagree with something.

2. Stories of people from literature, history, current events, or personal experience. For example, "My friend Sally thinks she isn't very pretty when really she's gorgeous. She would have a lot more confidence if she saw how beautiful she is."

Essay Prompt #2

1. Argumentative. You as a writer are trying to convince an audience of your point of view.

2. You could include studies citing why society, students, parents, or teachers would benefit from shorter school days or examples of how the current length of school day is detrimental to all of the above categories.

Essay Prompt #3

1. Descriptive. You do not have to convince anyone of anything, prove anything to anyone or otherwise support an argument, so what else is there left to do but describe something?

2. Stories of what happened while you were there, descriptions of landscapes, food, culture, and tourist sites. Also include why these places stand as your favorites over other places.

Essay Prompt #4

1. Open-ended. It asks you to "examine" which is another way of saying "come up with your own point of view."

2. Relevant English and American historical events and how they fed into American Independence, discussions of personalities within that history and how they influenced outcomes large and small.

Brainstorming

Brainstorming is when you quickly think up as many ideas as possible related to a certain topic. Your only goal is to come up with quantity. You are not editing or judging the ideas. You are just pouring from your mind as many thoughts as possible.

At the end of this lesson, you will be able to:

- understand how to use brainstorming in the writing process
- brainstorm extensively on an essay assignment

Parent's Corner

Fifth graders can be quick thinking and spontaneous. When they receive a writing assignment, they may wish to go with their very first instinct and jump in immediately. As a parent, it's important to check that your student has considered all possible options in writing topics. Challenge them to brainstorm more and think outside the box! Ask them if their chosen topic has enough examples and supporting evidence to carry the entire essay.

Dive Right In!

Prepared Examples

Directions: Come up with "prepared example" topics you could use in an essay. These should be general examples that you could have "prepared" in your back pocket if you are asked to write an essay. Some examples could include instances of great courage, an example of a parent-child relationship, an example of friendship, or an example of a difficult journey you or someone you know may have experienced. To get you brainstorming, try to think of events from history, literature, current events, or your own life. Answers will vary.

1.

2.

3.

4.

5.

6.

Sample answers can be found on page 120.

Explore

Where Do You Start?

When you have to write an essay, what process do you follow? How do you begin? What obstacles do you encounter? Remember the last time you had to write an essay and how that experience unfolded. Fill in this chart with your personal writing process. Be honest. Step 1 should be the first thing you do after you read the essay prompt or question.

Your Writing Process	Description	Possible Problem
Step 1		
Step 2		
Step 3		
Step 4		
Step 5		

Let's see how brainstorming can help you focus an essay. First, read this essay assignment.

⇨ *Top professional athletes and entertainers can earn millions of dollars a year. Although many protest the celebrities' salaries, they deserve what they earn.*

Assignment: What is your opinion of the claim that celebrity salaries are justified? Plan and write an essay in which you develop your point of view on this issue. Support your position with reasoning and examples taken from your reading, studies, experiences, or observations.

Before you decide whether you agree or disagree, brainstorm arguments for both sides and record them in the following chart. Write down as many examples as possible for each side. Don't worry about whether they are good examples or if they are well written right now. Just write!

Celebrities Deserve Their Large Salaries	
Agree	**Disagree**

Supporting Details

Now that you have your examples, think about what makes an example powerful. What is going to make each example a strong one? Let's say your argument is that cats are better pets than dogs and that one of your examples is that cats are cleaner than dogs. How are you going to prove that cats are cleaner? You can't just say so! You're going to need **supporting details.** Supporting details include specific information like names, dates, events, stories, and examples that *show* how your thesis is true in real life. What is a supporting detail for why cats are cleaner than dogs?

Reread the essay assignment about celebrity salaries on the previous page. Try to add as many supporting details as you can for each of the examples. Write the examples and details in the following charts:

Agree with Large Salaries		Disagree with Large Salaries	
Example	**Supporting Details**	**Example**	**Supporting Details**

Now that you've written as many supporting details as possible, look through your examples and choose the three strongest ones. The strongest examples will be the examples with the most supporting details. In other words, the strongest example is the example that has the most support. Circle those three examples.

Why would you prepare examples for an essay on a test ahead of time? Preparing examples ahead of time lets you spend more time writing and less time thinking of examples! If you prepare ahead of time, then you'll have a bank of knowledge to draw from. To boost your score, you can memorize extras like quotations, dates, event details, and authors.

But how can you plan examples if you don't know the essay assignment? Often, essay assignments on standardized tests revolve around universal themes like loss, progress, future, fairness, honesty, education, or experience. Many well-known events in history, like World War I, Helen Keller's life, or Ghandi's mission, will cover several of these areas. By coming to a test with examples in mind, you have more control over the essay and can shape your example to the given assignment. It's best to choose examples from history, literature, science, or current events.

Participate

Activity: Hands-On

Gather colored pencils, crayons, markers, pens, and any other craft supplies, and create a colorful, interesting-to-look-at brainstorm of your favorite summertime activities, favorite weekend activities, or favorite foods and tastes.

In a Nutshell

Skills

- **Brainstorming** for an essay is thinking of as many ideas as possible without judging them. The goal is quantity over quality.

- After you come up with examples, write down **supporting details** for each one.

- Choose the strongest examples based on the quality of the supporting details.

- Remember to come up with examples *before* you take a side!

Answers for Dive Right In:

Answers may vary.

The following are examples of what to include in a prepared example:

- a well-known subject with recognizable themes
- new information on a familiar topic
- inventive analysis or arguments tying the larger work to a theme
- ability to include details like dates, names, and descriptions of events
- relevant quotations

Crafting a Thesis Statement

A **thesis statement** is your essay's argument. The thesis, a debatable point, is different from the main idea, which is the topic, and from the summary, which is a list of facts. Ask yourself what you are going to convince the reader of by the end of the essay. The answer is your thesis.

At the end of this lesson, you will be able to:

- recognize the difference between thesis statements, opinions, and facts

- understand how to build a good thesis statement

- create well-written thesis statements

Parent's Corner

Learning how to write an effective thesis statement is among the most important skills your student will learn in fifth grade. It is crucial that they understand what a thesis statement actually is. Help them differentiate between a thesis statement and a *topic* of an essay. One important test of your child's thesis is whether or not it is debatable or not. A good thesis is not just a fact. If they tell you their thesis is something like "The War of 1812 was an important war between the United States and Great Britain," they haven't really written a thesis, since that statement isn't really in dispute. A better version would be "The War of 1812 was an important war because it ushered in new military technology and signaled for the United States a clean break with its old nemesis Great Britain." Challenge your student to write theses that can be *debated*.

Dive Right In!

Both Sides of the Fence

Directions: Read the following quote by Ralph Waldo Emerson:

"A hero is no braver than an ordinary man, but he is braver five minutes longer."

Do you agree or disagree? Support your position with examples from literature, current events, history, science, or personal experience.

1.   Agree thesis:

2.   Disagree thesis:

3.   Analyze the reason thesis:

4.   Cause and effect thesis:

Trade with a partner and suggest ways the other person could strengthen the thesis statements. Rewrite your own thesis statements based on your partner's suggestions. Answers will vary.

Sample responses can be found on page 130.

Explore

Opinions, Thesis Statements, and Facts

The challenge of writing a good thesis statement is to make sure it is a logical argument, provable with facts. A thesis is neither a fact nor an opinion. It's in the middle of the two.

Opinion————————Thesis————————Fact

Take a look at the following sentences. Write down whether you think they are opinions, thesis statements, or facts.

1. Music fans should show their support for their favorite musicians by purchasing their albums rather than by downloading music illegally from the Internet.

2. Over the past century, noise and light pollution have increased in tandem with the world's population and technological advances.

3. Although many people think animal testing is unethical, it is necessary in order for scientists to develop cures for human diseases.

Crafting a Solid Thesis Statement

Let's take a look at two possible ways to create a great thesis statement and avoid the pitfalls of the opinion/fact trap.

Cause and Effect Thesis

Consider writing a cause and effect essay. To write a **cause and effect thesis**, simply fill in this formula: The author/person/character uses _____ to show/because/for the purpose of _____. The first blank is an idea or way something happened. The second blank is the result or the consequences of that idea. For example,

⇨ In *Adventures of Huckleberry Finn*, Mark Twain uses the relationship between the slave Jim and the boy Huck to show that it is possible for the two cultures to connect and evolve together.

⇨ President Harry S. Truman's decision to drop the atomic bomb in World War II was necessary to prevent the deaths of even more civilians and soldiers.

Analyze the Reason Thesis

A cause and effect thesis examines what happens *after* or because of an action. An **analyze the reason thesis** examines what happens *before* or causes an action. Think about the reasons behind why fictional stories, historical moments, current events, cultural beliefs, or societal trends happen in the way they do. Underline the motivations for the actions taken in these situations. The motivation is the argument, or thesis.

4. The main reason Americans diet is to lengthen their lifespans.

5. Social reformer and 1872 presidential candidate Victoria Woodhull went to extremes in her life to raise awareness for the women's suffrage movement.

Answers can be found on page 130.

Thesis Quality Control

How do you know if you have a strong thesis? Ask yourself these questions.

Question 1: Could someone use facts to argue logically against my thesis?

Question 2: Can my thesis both be proved and disproved?

If you answer yes to both questions, then you have a strong thesis. Look at these three sample thesis statements and fill in the chart.

Sample Thesis Statement	Is the thesis strong?	Why?
I think cats might be better pets than dogs.		
I like cats better than dogs.		
Cats are better pets than dogs.		
There are more pet cats in this country than pet dogs.		

From Brainstorming to Thesis

If you can both prove *and* disprove a thesis statement, how do you decide which direction to pick? Which thesis statement will make a stronger essay? This is where brainstorming is helpful. Never pick a thesis without brainstorming first. You want to make sure you have enough logical examples and supporting details for your chosen thesis. The only way to make sure you have enough facts is to go through the brainstorming process for both sides of a potential thesis. In the last chapter, you brainstormed your ideas about this prompt.

⇨ *Top professional athletes and entertainers can earn millions of dollars a year. Although many protest celebrities' salaries, they deserve what they earn.*

Assignment: What is your opinion of the claim that celebrity salaries are justified? Plan and write an essay in which you develop your point of view on this issue. Support your position with reasoning and examples taken from your reading, studies, experiences, or observations.

Now that you've reread the assignment, reexamine how you chose your three strongest examples. Using the brainstorming process will make writing thesis statements much easier! Look at the three examples you chose for the celebrity salaries prompt in the last chapter. Would you still choose the same examples? Of the ones you chose, do more fall into the agree category or the disagree category? Whichever one has the strongest examples will determine your point of view and, ultimately, your thesis.

6. Based on your examples, do you agree or disagree that celebrities deserve their large salaries?

7. Write a strong, clear, and concise thesis statement stating this point of view.

8. List your three examples and their supporting details.

ONE MORE THING... The most compelling writing has a point and sticks to it. Everyone you'll work with in life—most especially teachers, college admissions officers, bosses, and clients—prefers to read concise writing in which the argument is apparent. No one likes struggling to understand someone's writing, so make your argument clear from the start and follow it with strong, relevant support.

Participate

Activity: Hands-On

Imagine that you want to convince your parents or an adult to buy you a new video game or toy or bike. Brainstorm a formal presentation that you might give, in order to convince them to buy this item for you. First, craft a thesis statement. Try creating a few different statements to work for this argument.

In a Nutshell

Skills

- A **thesis statement** is your essay's argument. The thesis, a debatable point, is different from the main idea and from the summary.

- A strong thesis statement can be argued for and against with facts. You should be able to both prove and disprove your thesis.

- Two possible ways to approach a thesis statement are to "analyze the reason" for an event or to write a "cause and effect" thesis, where you cite both the event and the results of the event.

Answers for Dive Right In:

Here are some possible answers:

1. Agree: As Ralph Waldo Emerson argues, heroes prove themselves by being braver longer than anyone else.

2. Disagree: Ralph Waldo Emerson is wrong about the nature of a hero; a hero is indeed braver than ordinary people.

3. Analyze the Reason: The reason heroes are braver longer is because they are the last ones standing when a situation becomes unbearable.

4. In *At the Earth's Core*, David is a hero because he is braver longer than anyone else.

 Answers for Explore:

1. Opinion

2. Fact

3. Thesis

4. To lengthen their life spans

5. To raise awareness for the women's suffrage movement

Organizing the Essay

Like everything in life, writing great essays takes practice. In this chapter, we'll summarize the process for you all in one place for easy reference.

At the end of this lesson, you will be able to:

- understand how to write and organize an essay
- organize and write your own essay
- format an essay appropriately

Parent's Corner

Even though writing an essay can seem like a laborious task for fifth graders, help them understand the creativity in the process. You, as the writer, have an exciting array of options in how to organize your essay. Encourage the process of writing several drafts, pushing students to see how much better their work can be with rewriting and reorganizing.

Dive Right In!

Write About Reality

Directions: Write an essay responding to this prompt:

Do you think reality television is representative of reality? Why or why not?

Use your knowledge of how to organize the essay, how to make the introduction and conclusion leave lasting impressions on the reader, and how to effectively use transitions. After you have written the essay, give it to a partner to read and comment on. Answers will vary.

_____

_____

_____

_____

_____

_____

_____

_____

_____

_____

Explore

The Planning Process

Step 1: Strategize. Determine the **type of essay assignment** and the kind of writing expected from you. Use this information to plan a time frame for yourself. Even if you only have twenty minutes to write the essay on an exam, take two minutes to plan.

Step 2: Brainstorm. Come up with as many ideas as you can about the topic. Don't judge them. Here, quantity is more important than quality!

Step 3: Fill In. After brainstorming, organize the ideas into categories and different possible responses to the essay prompt. Find **supporting details** for each example.

For an essay in which you're asked to agree or disagree with a statement, use this chart to organize your ideas.

Agree with Statement		Disagree with Statement	
Example	Supporting Details	Example	Supporting Details

Step 4: Create a thesis statement. A thesis statement is your essay's argument. Look at your strongest examples and supporting details from your brainstorming session. What debatable point will you argue? Ask yourself these two questions to make sure your thesis is a good one.

1.   Could someone use facts to argue logically against your thesis?
2.   Can your thesis both be proved and disproved?

The Writing Process

Step 1: Using your examples and supporting details, start writing your **body paragraphs**. Remember your thesis at all times. Keep the writing tight by varying sentence structure and transitions. Body paragraphs should have the following elements:

- an opening sentence that introduces the paragraph's topic

- necessary supporting details

- a concluding sentence that summarizes the details

- transitions at the beginning of the paragraph, between details, and at the end of the paragraph

Step 2: After writing your body paragraphs, reread them. Use their content to design your **introduction**. Your introduction should include these elements.

- motivation for your audience to read the essay

- background information and context for your argument

- the thesis proved by your body paragraphs

Step 3: Writing the **conclusion** is the final step of the writing process. Your conclusion must do three things.

- restate the thesis

- summarize briefly the most important facts proving the thesis

- connect the essay to the reader's life or experience

Formatting

Many teachers are very specific about format when they assign an essay. They'll tell you how many pages or how many words are required, if you need a bibliography and what kind, if it needs to be typed, and more.

Bottom line: **Always follow the directions.**

The teacher wrote the assignment with a purpose. He or she wants to see certain elements in your writing and creates the assignment's format accordingly. Use the assignment information to your advantage. Reference it frequently while writing. Aim to write for your audience. What kind of work does the teacher expect? To do well, determine what the teacher wants and deliver it. If you're not sure, ask and listen closely to the answer. Take careful notes to remember the instructions.

If your paper is too short, write more. Add another body paragraph. Insert more supporting details. When typing, avoid changing the font style, font size, space between lines, or margins. Teachers will be able to tell. When in doubt, type with a twelve-point standard word-processing font, use one-inch margins, and double space.

Again, always follow the directions!

ONE MORE THING... How do you learn to play an instrument or speak another language? You follow a process. As with learning music and languages, learning to write well means following steps. Think about the saying, "Learn the rules before you break them." When you know how to play the guitar, you can experiment to create unique, new music. When you fully understand the nuances of a language, you can make jokes and communicate with people in a much deeper way. The same is true of writing. Once you have mastered the process, you can write more creative and insightful essays. Instead of worrying about *how* you're going to write your essays, you can focus on *what* you will write.

 **Participate**

Activity: Hands-On

Grab some paper and write a short essay. Use the prompt below as the subject.

Do you agree/disagree that...in order to be successful you need to break some rules?

In a Nutshell

Skills

The Planning Process

- **Step 1:** Determine the type of essay assignment and the kind of writing expected from you. Use this information to plan a time frame for yourself.
- **Step 2:** Brainstorm. Come up with as many ideas as you can about the topic. Here, quantity is more important than quality!
- **Step 3:** After brainstorming, organize the ideas into categories and different possible responses to the essay prompt. Find supporting details for each example.
- **Step 4:** Create a thesis statement. A thesis statement is your essay's argument.

The Writing Process

- **Step 1:** Using your examples and supporting details, start writing your body paragraphs. Keep your thesis in mind at all times.
- **Step 2:** After writing your body paragraphs, reread them. Use their content to design your introduction.
- **Step 3:** Finally, write the conclusion.

Math

All About Numbers
Working with Numbers
Math in Real Life

Number Families

On your last trip to the department store, the store managers hoped you would find exactly what you needed. Why? Because they want your business! So they designed the layout of the store to make it very easy for you to find and buy those items and, they hope, a few others.

What does this have to do with math?

By separating items into different categories, we can locate and use them more easily. Were you looking for a new shirt? Go to the clothing department. Want some towels? Check out the linens department. This same logic applies to the numbers we see every day.

Like department stores, numbers have their own categories. Numbers can fall into one or more categories, so it's important to know how groups of numbers break down into smaller groups. Most math and science books will talk about these families, so it's important to know about them.

At the end of this lesson, you will be able to:

- identify the possible families for any number
- use variables to represent any number

Parent's Corner

Fifth graders may be used to thinking as math as simply "numbers." This is the time to help them parse out what they really mean: what kind of number specifically? A whole number, decimal, integer, negative? As their math curriculum develops, their math vocabulary will need to develop with it.

Dive Right In!

Number Families

Directions: Using words, define what the math terms are in the "What They Are" column. Then write what they are not by listing the types of numbers not included in their category. Using numbers, write three examples of each under the column named "Examples."

Term	What They Are	What They Are Not	Examples
whole numbers			
integers			
rational numbers			
irrational numbers			
real numbers			
constant numbers			
variables			

Answers can be found on page 148.

Explore

Whole Numbers

Let's start with numbers that pop up the most in your everyday life. Think of a number. You probably thought of a **whole number.** Some examples of whole numbers are 0, 1, 2, 3, 57, and 948. Whole numbers consist of the type of number you can count out starting with 0.

In the space below, list five whole numbers that haven't been mentioned.

Integers

Whole numbers and their negatives make up the group called **integers**. Integers are numbers you see on a number line: positive, negative, and 0. Integers extend infinitely in both the positive and negative directions on the number line. Fractions and decimals are *not* included in this category.

Circle the integers in this list of numbers.

$$3 \qquad 17 \qquad -9.35 \qquad -101 \qquad 0 \qquad \frac{13}{2}$$

Rational Numbers

Numbers that can be written as fractions (an integer over an integer) are called

rational numbers. For example, $\frac{2}{3}$, $\frac{10}{7}$, and $\frac{4}{5}$ are all rational numbers. Integers are

also rational numbers because they can be written as themselves over 1; for example,

12 can be rewritten as $\frac{12}{1}$, so it's a rational number.

Irrational Numbers

Numbers that cannot be rewritten as fractions are called **irrational numbers**. Some good examples of irrational numbers are $\sqrt{2}$, $\sqrt{3}$, and π. Roots that can't be reduced are irrational.

Many people say that π is $\dfrac{22}{7}$ or 3.14. However, although $\dfrac{22}{7}$ or 3.14 is close, it is only an approximation, and it is slightly larger than the actual value of π.

Label the following numbers as either rational or irrational.

$$\frac{1}{3} \qquad -19 \qquad \sqrt{5} \qquad -0.2 \qquad 0.5 \qquad -\sqrt{7}$$

Real Numbers

All the numbers that we've been talking about so far are **real numbers**. The real numbers consist of whole numbers, integers, rational numbers, and irrational numbers. Real numbers can be anything except for the even root of a negative number. Real numbers include 3, 0.7, and $\dfrac{1}{2}$. However, $\sqrt{-3}$, $\sqrt[6]{-36}$, and $\sqrt[100]{-100}$ are not real numbers.

Constants

Constant numbers are numbers that don't change. All the numbers that we've talked about so far are constants. This category also includes those unusual numbers like π, which you'll learn about later.

Variables

Variables represent unknown numbers. A great example is *x*, which often represents any number. These unknown numbers are the opposite of constants, which are known and don't change; variables are unknown and can change.

Label the following numbers as constant or variable.

$$3xy \qquad 17x^2 \qquad -x\sqrt{5} \qquad 0.71 \qquad \frac{3a}{7} \qquad -\sqrt{19} \qquad \frac{7}{8}$$

Answers can be found on page 148.

When cashiers give you change, they are handling real, rational numbers. Many people, such as scientists and engineers, work with constants and variables. Crime-scene investigators use formulas full of variables to figure out mysteries. You can see number families in action everywhere.

Participate

Activity: Hands-On

Open a math text book to a random page. Go through every number on that page, number by number, and say out loud if the number is a whole number , an integer, a rational number, an irrational number, a real number, a constant, a variable, or maybe a few of those things at the same time.

In a Nutshell

Definitions

- **Whole Numbers:** counting numbers, including 0, 2, and 12

- **Integers:** positive and negative whole numbers, such as −6, 0, and 7

- **Rational Numbers:** numbers that can be represented as fractions, like $\frac{2}{3}$, $\frac{4}{1}$, and $\frac{7}{2}$

- **Irrational Numbers:** numbers that cannot be written as fractions, like $\sqrt{2}$ and π

- **Real Numbers:** all of the above; nearly anything can be a real number, except for negative roots, such as $\sqrt{-3}$

- **Variables:** letters used in the place of a constant number when the value is unknown or could change

A · Answers for Dive Right In:

- **Whole Numbers**—ARE counting numbers that include zero; ARE NOT decimals, fractions, or negative numbers
  Examples: 0, 1, 5, 12, 31

- **Integers**—ARE whole numbers and their negatives; ARE NOT decimals or fractions
  Examples: –35, –1, 0, 1, 3, 17, 412

- **Rational Numbers**—ARE numbers that can be written as a fraction (an integer over an integer); ARE NOT square roots or π
  Examples: $-\dfrac{4}{5}$, –2, 0, $\dfrac{12}{17}$, 2.5, 4.125

- **Irrational Numbers**—ARE numbers that cannot be written as a fraction such as nonreducible square roots and π; ARE NOT fractions, whole numbers, integers, or rational numbers
  Examples: $-2\sqrt{3}$, $\sqrt{5}$, π

- **Real Numbers**—ARE whole numbers, integers, rational numbers, and irrational numbers; ARE NOT even roots of negative numbers
  Examples: π, –19, 0, $\dfrac{3}{2}$, 1.8, $\sqrt{7}$

- **Constants**—ARE numbers that are known and don't change, such as all of the above terms; this category also includes those unusual numbers like π and e; ARE NOT unknown numbers that change
  Examples: –8, 0, 1, $\dfrac{3}{2}$, π, 5.75

- **Variables**—ARE unknown numbers that change; ARE NOT constant numbers
  Examples: p, q, r, x, y, z

A · Answers for Explore:

3	integer
17	integer
–9.35	not an integer
–101	integer
0	integer
$\dfrac{13}{2}$	not an integer
$\dfrac{1}{3}$	rational
–19	rational
$\sqrt{5}$	irrational
–0.2	rational
0.5	rational
$-\sqrt{7}$	irrational
$3xy$	variable
e	constant
$17x^2$	variable
$-x\sqrt{5}$	variable
0.71	constant
$\dfrac{3a}{7}$	variable
$-\sqrt{19}$	constant
$\dfrac{7}{8}$	constant

Number Lines and Inequalities

You might not realize it, but you have been using number lines for a long time. Whenever you check a thermometer to find the temperature or turn the oven on to start cooking, you are using a number line to discover something. **Number lines** show the relationships between numbers and help you visualize operations such as addition and subtraction.

How would you find out which number is greater: $\frac{3}{8}$ or $\frac{1}{4}$? One way is to look at a ruler, a type of number line.

At the end of this lesson, you will be able to:

- create and read number lines

- use number lines to show inequalities

- use number lines to show negative values

- use number lines to show addition and subtractions

Parent's Corner

The number line is a great visual tool to help your fifth grader understand math (particularly if the student is a visual learner). Consider having an arts and crafts day with your student: can you draw your own number line and put it up somewhere in your home? Make sure to include negative numbers as well. This small step can help your child get more comfortable and familiar with numbers.

Dive Right In!

Throwing a Party

Directions: You are planning to host a surprise party at your house for your best friend. After gathering donations from friends on the guest list, you have $100 to spend. Each question below gives you a choice of expenses. Determine how you want to spend your money and mark each number line accordingly.

1. You start with $100. Mark it.

2. Food: Choose between spending $30 for pizza or $40 for hot dogs, hamburgers, and the toppings. Depending on what you choose, mark and label how much money you have left.

3. Drinks: Choose between spending $15 for soda or $20 for ice cream and fruit to make smoothies. Depending on what you choose, mark and label how much money you have left.

4. Music: Choose between downloading music for the party off the Internet for $20 or hiring a friend's band to perform for $50. Depending on what you choose, mark and label how much money you have left. (It's okay to go lower than 0.)

5. Decorations: Choose between banners saying "Surprise!" for $5 or a bunch of helium balloons for $15. Depending on what you choose, mark and label how much money you have left.

6. Did you spend more than $100?

7. If yes, how much more? If not, how much less?

8. Which expense would you cut in order to stick to your budget?

9. Why is creating a number line useful for this kind of planning?

Sample answers can be found on page 158.

Explore

Properties of Number Lines

A number line is a picture that evenly spaces numbers in order, usually from smallest to largest. Here is a number line that shows the numbers 0 through 9 in order from smallest to largest.

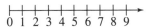

We call 0 the **origin,** because that's where this (and many other) number lines start. The arrow on the right side of the number line saves space. It shows that there are numbers after 9, but it allows you to express this without having to write them out.

A football field is a number line with a nonzero origin. The origin is the 50-yard line in the middle, and it counts down to 0 at each end.

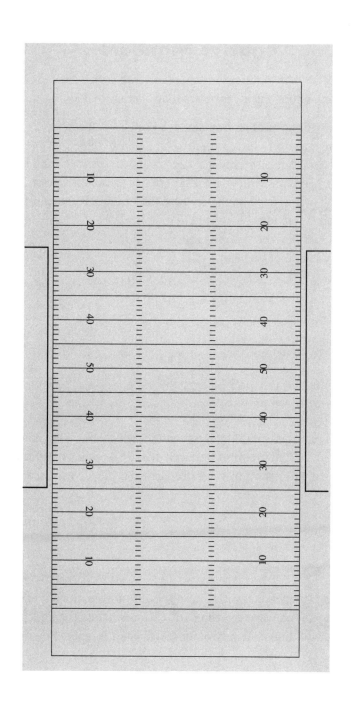

Positive and Negative Numbers

Number lines explain how different numbers relate to each other. For instance, you can tell if the temperature outside is hotter than average by looking at a thermometer.

A thermometer is a basic number line that everyone uses at some point. But not every day is warm enough to be represented on a number line that starts with 0 and increases. In the Celsius measurement system, water freezes at 0° and boils at 100°. If you trek through Alaska in winter, you'll experience Celsius temperatures far below 0°. Zero is still the origin, because that's where the number line begins, even though it extends in opposite directions.

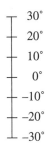

A minus sign (−) represents numbers less than 0°, which are called **negative numbers**. A positive sign (+) indicates numbers greater than 0°, or **positive numbers**. If a number line does not provide a positive or negative sign, you can assume the numbers are positive.

Inequalities

Notice that the farther away a positive number is from zero, the larger it is. Thus, we say that 30° is larger (and warmer!) than 10°. This is what mathematicians mean when they talk about **inequalities**—that two numbers, when compared on a number line, are not equal.

But what about comparing +20° and −20°? These two numbers are **opposites,** because they are the same number, but they have different signs (+ and −). From the example above we can see that +20° and −20° are the same size, or the same distance, from zero. So how do we compare them? Most number lines are arranged from smallest to largest, or **least** to **greatest**. On a horizontal number line, the least numbers will be on the left and the greatest will be on the right. On a vertical number line, the least numbers will be on the bottom and the greatest will be on the top.

Inequality Signs

To show that the left number is **larger** than the right number, use the **greater than sign: >** .

$$20° > -20°$$

To show that the left number is **smaller** than the right number, use the **less than sign: <** .

$$-20° < 20°$$

Mnemonic Devices

Mnemonic devices are tricks to help you remember something. Here are a few helpful ways to remember which inequality sign is which.

1. Use the directions of the arrows on the number line to help you remember. The arrow at the bigger end of the number line means *greater than* and the arrow at the smaller end means *less than*.

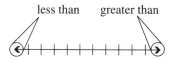

2. Think of the sign in the middle of the inequality as an arrow pointing to the smaller number.

$$5 > 3 \text{ becomes } 5 \rightarrow 3$$
$$3 < 5 \text{ becomes } 3 \leftarrow 5$$

3. You may have learned this last way a long time ago: Think of the inequality signs as hungry alligators with their mouths open—naturally they want to eat the bigger number. As a hungry alligator, which would you prefer: 7 or 2? 7 of course! Thus, 7 > 2 and 2 < 7. Sometimes the silliest memory devices work best!

Addition on a Number Line

We can also show addition on a number line. For example, the equation 2 + 2 = 4 translates into the following form:

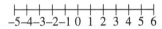

If you start at the origin and draw two lines, each two units long, side by side along a number line, they extend to the number 4. Any addition problem can be represented in this way. We start at the origin because it is the beginning of this number line.

Draw 1 + 4 on this number line. Circle the correct answer. Remember to start at 0!

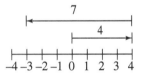

Subtraction on a Number Line

Subtraction works in a similar way. Because you can get negative answers, you need to have a number line with negative numbers! Let's draw 4 − 7 = −3 on this number line.

Start at the origin, move right 4 places, and then move left 7 places to end at −3, the answer to the equation.

ONE MORE THING... We are surrounded by number lines and use them all the time. Gas meters, speedometers, thermometers, and rulers are all number lines. A football field is an enormous number line, visible from the sky!

Participate

Activity: Hands-On 1

Write a list of the places where you see number lines in your day-to-day life.

1._____

2._____

3._____

Activity: Hands-On 2

Write out a list of your opinions using the less than or greater than signs.

Examples: Bananas > grapes (I love bananas!)

Saturday > Monday (I live for weekends!)

Rap music > Rock and Roll (rap forever!)

In a Nutshell

Definitions

- **Number Line:** a group of numbers written out in order on a line

- **Origin:** the beginning of a number line, often 0

- **Opposite:** numbers that are the same distance from the origin, such as −5 and 5

- **Inequality:** a way of comparing two numbers or expressions

- **"Less Than" Sign (<):** used to show that one number is smaller than another

- **"Greater Than" Sign (>):** used to show that one number is larger than another

- **Positive Number:** a number greater than 0

- **Negative Number:** a number less than 0, shown with a negative sign, like −9

 Sample answers for Dive Right In:

1. Mark $100 on the number line.

2. Say you choose the $30 pizza, so 100 − 30 = 70 remaining. Mark $70 on the number line.

3. Say you choose the $15 soda option, so 70 − 15 = 55. Mark $55 on the number line.

4. Say you choose the $20 internet option, so 55 − 20 = 35. Mark $35 on the number line.

5. Say you choose the $5 "Surprise" banner, so 35 − 5 = 30. Mark $30 on the number line.

6. In this case, you've NOT spent more than $100.

7. In this case, you've spent $70, or $30 less than $100.

8. Answers will vary about what should be cut from the budget if you went over $100.

9. Yes! The number line is helpful so we can stay on budget!

Properties of Zero

Little did you know that all the time you spent playing at the playground when you were young was preparing you to do math. One of the toys there both let you have fun *and* taught you: the seesaw, also called a teeter-totter. A seesaw is a plank centered on a base so that each side of the plank is of equal length. Think of **zero** as the base of the seesaw. It sits in the middle on the number line. It balances the number line, but it's not like the other numbers. It has rules all its own.

In math, we often need to talk about nothingness, so we have a name for it: zero.

At the end of this lesson, you will be able to:

- understand how zero behaves

- know how and when to use zero

Parent's Corner

Help drive home the importance of zero to your student. Make sure to quiz them on two very important rules: anything divided by zero is undefined (i.e. we can *never* divide by 0) and zero divided by anything is zero (i.e. $\frac{4}{0} = 0$, $-\frac{11}{0} = 0$.).

Dive Right In!

Properties of Zero

Directions: Determine whether the following equations are true or false. If a statement is false, state the rule explaining why it is false.

1. $-3(0) = -3$

2. $4 + 16 + 0 = 21$

3. $7(0) - 5 = -5$

4. $\dfrac{42}{0} = 0$

5. $89 - 0(4) = 85$

6. $\dfrac{0}{100} = 0$

Answers can be found on page 166.

Explore

Zero

Zero is a great number! Sometimes it acts like other numbers, and sometimes it doesn't. In order to better understand zero, think of it as the doorway between two rooms. The rooms themselves have their own furniture and walls and decorations. Although the doorway is connected to those rooms, it is its own separate piece. On a number line, zero sits in the middle between the positive numbers and negative numbers, but **zero is neither positive nor negative.** You can also think of it as nothingness, or absence of numbers. What happened if you sat on the center of the seesaw? Nothing!

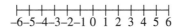

Let's take a quick look at that number line we spoke about earlier. Which are the even numbers?

Notice that every other number is even. If you look at this pattern, what do you notice about zero? That's right, **zero is even.**

What Can Zero Do?

What happens when you add nothing to something? Nothing. Let's use numbers as an example. What happens when you add 0 to 4?

What happens if you subtract? If you take nothing from 4, or calculate 4 – 0, what do you get?

What if you have 0 – 4?

Multiplication

Multiplying is the same as adding a number over and over again. What happens when you add a number no times?

Let's take an example: What is 7×0? It's 0, because there are no 7s added. Now, let's flip this idea of multiplication. What is 0×7? It's still 0, because 7 sets of nothing is still nothing.

Therefore, anything times 0 is 0.

An even number is a number that can be divided by 2 with no remainder. Does this work with zero? Why or why not?

Division

Now let's talk about dividing with zero. Division is breaking something down into equal parts. When you split a group into two teams for a basketball game, you're dividing the group by 2. Another way to think about it is, "How many times can I take a certain number out of a group?" For example, if the question is $32 \div 8$, the question is really asking how many 8s you can pull out of 32? The answer is 4.

Now let's think about this idea with zero. If the question is $0 \div 4$, what is the question really asking?

Answer the question you posed:

Once again, you've come up with a rule: **Zero divided by anything is zero**.

What Can't Zero Do?

So what about the opposite? What happens when you flip the idea of division? What happens when you try to find any number divided by zero? It's a trick question. You can't do it! It doesn't work. Let's examine why.

Another way to think of division is that it's the opposite of multiplication. So $8 \div 2$ is 4, because 4×2 is 8.

Let's talk about this idea using zero: Let's say $15 \div 0$ is x. So this would mean that $x \times 0$ is 15. But we already know that anything times 0 is 0, not 15 or any other number. So it doesn't work to divide numbers by 0. When something doesn't work in math, it's described as **undefined**.

What is $24 \div 0$?

Why?

What is $\dfrac{0}{0}$?

Answers can be found on page 166.

Quick Recap

- Zero is neither positive nor negative.
- Zero is even.
- Zero added to any number is that number.
- Any number minus zero is that number.
- Zero plus a negative number (another way of saying subtraction) is that negative number.
- Zero times anything is zero.
- Anything times zero is zero.
- Zero divided by anything is zero.
- Anything divided by zero is undefined.

ONE MORE THING... Zero can be a great help when it comes to math problems. You're working hard to solve a really long, difficult multiplication problem and you realize that it's all being multiplied by zero. Man, all that work for nothing—literally! Now the answer is just zero. Keep your eye out for zero, because sometimes you'll see it in a really complex problem that you don't actually have to solve. The question may just be testing your knowledge of the rules and properties of zero.

Participate

Activity: Hands-On

Clap along and sing a song, number by number, about the serious power of zero!

$9 \times 0 = 0$

$8 \times 0 = 0$

Etc.

$9 \div 0 = 0$

$8 \div 0 = 0$

Etc.

In a Nutshell

Definitions

- Zero: the placeholder that separates the positive from the negative numbers

- Undefined: the result of dividing by zero

Rules

- 0 is neither positive nor negative.

- 0 is even.

- $anything \times 0 = 0$

- $\dfrac{0}{anything} = 0$

Hints

- Anything divided by 0 is undefined. If you find yourself doing this to solve a problem, check to see if there is an error in your math somewhere.

Answers for Dive Right In:

1. False. Anything times zero is zero. So the result is zero.

2. False. Zero added to any number is that number. $4 + 16 = 20$; and, $20 + 0 = 20$.

3. True. Zero times any number is zero. Zero plus a negative number is that negative number.

4. False. Anything divided by zero is undefined.

5. False. Anything times zero is zero. Zero added to any number is that number. So the answer would be 89.

6. True. Zero divided by anything is zero.

 Answers for Explore:

$24 \div 0$ is "undefined," for any of the above reasons.

$0 \div 0$ is technically "indeterminate," not undefined. Unlike other fractions with the same number on top and bottom, this is NOT equal to 1. Since the difference can only be explained with calculus, just tell your students to stick with the rule of thumb and *never divide by 0*.

Properties of One

In math, the number **1** represents a single thing. That unit can be anything: apples, temperature, points in a game, phones, songs. All numbers in the world are built with and begin with 1, so understanding 1 is essential.

At the end of this lesson, you will be able to:

- use the number 1 to simplify math

- become more comfortable with the basic properties of numbers

---

Parent's Corner

One is a powerful number, and we use it all the time. Try to go over the rules of 1 with your student: 3 times 1 is 3; 4 divided by 1 is 4, and 1 divided by 1 is 1.

Dive Right In!

One Thing or Many?

Directions: Think carefully about the following questions before answering. Then write detailed answers.

1. List as many ways as you can think of to divide the universe into groups.

    a. *alive and not alive*

    b. *the Periodic Table of Elements*

    c.

    d.

    e.

    f.

    g.

    h.

2. Do you think these groups can be reduced to one thing or many? Explain your answers.

   a. *alive and not alive—everything is made up of matter*

   b. *the Periodic Table of Elements—everything is made up of atoms*

   c.

   d.

   e.

   f.

   g.

   h.

Answers can be found on page 174.

Explore

Multiplication with One

First, you need to know how 1 interacts with other numbers. It usually simplifies things. In the following diagrams, we'll use a **variable**—a letter that can be used to represent any number—to show how to use 1. We'll use the letter n as our variable; n can stand for any number, and the equation will still be correct.

$$n \times 1 = n$$

Replace n with any number and the equation still works:

$$3 \times 1 = 3$$

Multiplication is another way of showing lots of addition. For instance, 2×4 is another way of saying $2 + 2 + 2 + 2$. When any number is multiplied by 1, you get that number as a result; there is nothing to add to it because you only want it to appear one time.

Division with One

$$\frac{n}{1} = n$$

Replace n with your favorite number and it will still work. For instance:

$$\frac{5}{1} = 5$$

Remember that division is the opposite of multiplication. Whereas multiplication asks you to add the same number over and over, division asks you to subtract the same number over and over. When something is divided by 1, as in the equation above, nothing is subtracted from the number.

$$\frac{n}{n} = 1$$

Remember that division is deciding how many groups of one number are in a different number? For example, a test problem might ask you how many groups of 4 you can divide a class of 20 students into: $20 \div 4 = 5$. But the answer is always the same when you divide a number by itself. How many groups of 7 are in 7? One!

You should note that 0 divided by 0 does not equal 1. In fact, it doesn't equal anything at all. We say that it is undefined—you just can't do it! Anything divided by 0 has no answer.

All the Rules of One

Here is a list of all the rules you need to know about 1:
- 1 times any number is that number.
- Any number divided by 1 is that number.
- Any number divided by itself is 1.
- 1 divided by any number is the reciprocal of that number.

Ones to Watch Out For

The number 1 can be tricky at times. It shows up so often that mathematicians sometimes don't write it; they just assume it. One also allows you to simplify certain equations. For example:

$$7 \times \left(\frac{5}{7} \right) = 7 \left(\frac{5}{7} \right) = \left(\frac{7}{7} \right) 5 = (1)5 = 5$$

ONE MORE THING... In the world of computers, 1 is the building block. Every picture, music file, game, or document on a computer is represented by a long string of 1s and 0s. One might be small, but it does a lot of work.

Participate

Activity: Hands-On

Do a 1 Walk: Walk around your home and point out things that come in 1, that you have 1 of. So you won't want to point at a bunch of grapes because that is more than 1, but as you walk, you might point at one painting hanging on a wall or one shirt folded up on a bed or one brush sitting on a dresser.

In a Nutshell

Rules

- $n \times 1 = n$

- $n \div 1 = n$

- $n \div n = 1$

- $1 \div n = \dfrac{1}{n}$

Answers for Dive Right In:

Here are some possible answers for Question 1:

• water, earth, air, wind, fire

• plant, animal, mineral

• Linnean (kingdom, phylum, class, order, family, genus, species)

• solid, liquid, gas

• countries/civilizations

• biomes

Question 2 answers may vary.

Multilplication

O ne way people count large amounts of similar objects, like a jar of change, is to split them into smaller groups and count the groups. For instance, you might have dumped out all of the change from the jar and separated the pennies into groups of 10 pennies each. If you had 9 groups of pennies, then you would know that you had 9 times 10, or 90, cents worth of pennies. You could use the same method on the nickels, dimes, and quarters in the jar. This is multiplication! What if you had a jar with 321 pennies, 42 nickels, 59 dimes, 22 quarters, and 6 dollar coins? How much money is in the jar?

At the end of this lesson, you will be able to:

- use multiplication to simplify adding large groups of similar things

- understand the different notations used for multiplication

Answer can be found on page 184.

Parent's Corner

Make sure your students are practicing multiplication as much as possible. Quiz them often, and have them quiz you back! You want them to be so comfortable with multiplication that they can instantly give you the answer to, say, 7 times 6.

Dive Right In!

Let Them Eat Brownies

Directions: Think about the following scenario and then answer the questions.

You are baking your famous brownies for a class party celebrating the last day of school. These ingredients make 24 brownies and, conveniently, there are 24 people in your math class. Another class of 24 hears about your party and wants to come, so you'll need to double the batch. How much of each of the ingredients listed below will you need in order to make 2 batches? What if your entire grade of 576 students wants to join in the fun? Fill in the chart!

To Feed 24 Students	To Feed 48 Students	To Feed 576 Students
$1\frac{1}{2}$ cups unsalted butter		
2 cups white sugar		
2 teaspoons vanilla extract		
7 eggs		

To Feed 24 Students	To Feed 48 Students	To Feed 576 Students
$1\frac{1}{3}$ cups all-purpose flour		
$1\frac{1}{2}$ cups unsweetened cocoa powder		
1 teaspoon salt		
1 pound chopped walnuts		

Answers can be found on page 184.

Explore

Multiplication

Multiplication is a short way to show large amounts of addition. For instance,

$$5 \times 7 \text{ means } 7 + 7 + 7 + 7 + 7$$

The first number tells you how many times you need to add the second number.

What is 4×3? Let's visualize an example. Imagine that your coach asked you to collect all the basketballs at the end of practice. If you can only carry 3 balls at a time and need to make 4 trips to get all the balls, how many balls are there?

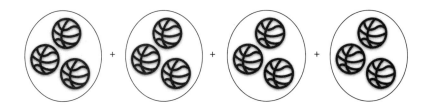

Count up the 4 groups of 3, and you'll find that the answer is 12.

Notation

Notation is a fancy name for the way you write something. There are a lot of different ways of writing multiplication.

- 2×4 is the first notation you probably learned.
- $2 \cdot 4$ is another way to show multiplication.
- (2)4 or 2(4) or (2)(4) is another common way to show multipication.
- 2*4 is used on calculators and computers.
- *ab* or *3a* is used with variables. When there is nothing between numbers and variables, or between variables and variables, they are being multiplied together.

Properties

Multiplication has a lot of properties that make it very flexible. This flexibility helps us change harder math problems into easier math problems.

Commutation

The **commutative property** of multiplication says that no matter what order a multiplication equation is in, the answer is always the same. Look at the picture of 4×3 and compare it with the picture of 3×4. Notice that in both cases there are 12 basketballs.

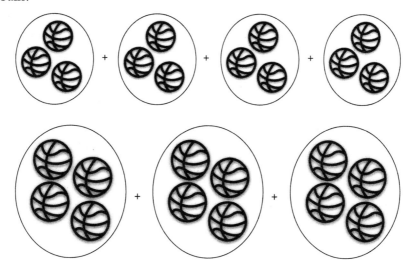

We're going to use **variables** to talk about multiplication from now on. You may recall that variables are letters that stand in for numbers when you don't know what the numbers are exactly. A variable could be any number. We will use a, b, and c.

So, we can say that the commutative property means

$$ab = ba$$

If a multiplication problem has more than one number, the commutative property still applies. For example,

$$3 \times 5 \times 7 = 3 \times 7 \times 5 = 5 \times 3 \times 7 = 5 \times 7 \times 3, \text{ and so on } \ldots$$

Distribution

When you combine addition and multiplication, there are times when you can spread, or distribute, the multiplication operation over the numbers being added. This is called the **distributive property** of multiplication. For instance,

$$7(a + b) = 7a + 7b$$

We can plug in some real numbers to show that this is true.

$$2(3 + 4) = 2(7) = 14$$
$$2(3 + 4) = 2(3) + 2(4) = 6 + 8 = 14$$

Multiplication with 1

Any number multiplied by 1 is equal to itself. What is 1 group of 6 basketballs? 6 basketballs!

So, we can say that

$$1 \times a = a$$

Multiplication with 0

Multiplying by 0 isn't difficult, because the sum of no numbers is 0! 0×7 means that there are no groups of 7. If there are no groups of 7, then there are no 7s at all. Therefore,

$$0 \times a = 0$$

Negative Numbers

Multiplication by negative numbers requires some memorization. When you multiply signs that are the same (like positive × positive), you get a positive answer. When the signs are different (negative × positive), you get a negative answer. Memorize these relationships!

positive × positive = positive
positive × negative = negative
negative × negative = positive

You can think about it this way: When a negative and a positive are multiplied together, there is nothing there to cancel out the negative, and it must remain in the answer. When two negatives are multiplied together, their negative signs cancel out. If it helps, you can think of the negative sign as a −1 and you can do anything to it that you would to a normal 1.

ONE MORE THING... Multiplication is an easier way to show difficult addition. It's also a quick way to count, among other things, the number of students in your class. If your desks are laid out in a rectangle, multiply the rows of desks by the columns of desks and you'll know how many students there are in class today. You can also use it to figure out how long each day at school is; if each class is 50 minutes long, and you have 6 classes, then you can multiply 6 times 50 to figure out how many minutes you spend in class each day.

Participate

Activity: Hands-On

Go into the kitchen and look at an item in the cupboard—it could be soup cans or Ramen packets or sugar packets or coffee filters. Count how many are in there. Then imagine if you used that many items every day for 7 days—how many would that be? What if you used that many items every day for 15 days—how many would that be? For 30 days? Do this multiplication as quickly as you can and do it without a calculator.

In a Nutshell

Definition

- **Multiplication:** a short way of showing a lot of addition

Rules

- $ab = ba$

- $a(b + c) = ab + ac$

- $1 \times a = a$

- $0 \times a = 0$

- When multiplying a positive number times a negative number, the answer is negative.

- When multiplying a negative number times a negative number, the answer is positive.

Answers for Opening Page:

The jar has $22.71 in change.

 Answers for Dive Right In:

For 48 students you will need:

3 cups of unsalted butter

4 cups of white sugar

4 teaspoons of vanilla extract

14 eggs

$2\frac{2}{3}$ cups of all-purpose flour

3 cups of unsweetened cocoa powder

2 teaspoons of salt

2 pounds of chopped walnuts

For 576 students you will need:

36 cups of unsalted butter

48 cups of white sugar

48 teaspoons of vanilla extract

168 eggs

32 cups of all-purpose flour

36 cups of unsweetened cocoa powder

24 teaspoons of salt

24 pounds of chopped walnuts

Division

Think of what goes into a yummy pizza: melting cheese, delicious toppings, tangy tomato sauce…and a math problem? Yes! All those wonderful slices of pizza do more than satisfy your hunger. They teach you about division. After all, how else can you make one pizza feed more than one person?

Likewise, imagine that your teacher has challenged you to a contest. If you can guess how many nickels are in a jar, you get to keep the whole jar and everything in it. Your teacher, being extra nice, tells you that the total money in the jar is $18.60. How many nickels are there?

At the end of this lesson, you will be able to:

- use division to simplify the subtraction of large groups of similar things

- understand the different notation used for division

- use division to undo multiplication

- use division to cut large numbers into smaller pieces

Answer can be found on page 196.

Parent's Corner

Help your fifth grader understand that division is nothing to be afraid of. It's simply the inverse of multiplication. If you can do multiplication, you can do division! Have your student solve division problems and multiplication problems back to back in order to solidify the relationship between the two.

Dive Right In!

A Night Out

Directions: Your parents and another couple go out to dinner. Everyone has agreed to pay for their share of the dinner. Here are the details:

2 people ordered salads for $7.95 each

3 people ordered burgers for $8.95 each

3 people ordered the chicken salad platter for $9.95 each

4 people ordered drinks at $1.50 each

4 people just drank water

Directions: Answer the problems using the above information.

1. Approximately what will the total order cost? Round!

2. Exactly what will the total be?

3. If tax is 8%, how much extra, in money, is tax? Use your answer for question 2.

4. What is the total with tax?

5. If you tip 15% on the exact total including tax, how much tip will you give?

6. What is the exact total order, including tax and tip?

7. How much will each person contribute if the total bill is divided evenly among the 4 adults?

Answers can be found on page 196.

Explore

Division as Subtraction

Division is the **inverse** of multiplication. That's a fancy way of saying that multiplication and division are opposites. When you multiply two numbers, you combine equal groups. When you **divide** something, you split a group into a number of equal portions. Whatever one can do, the other can undo. For instance,

$$5 \times 7 = 35$$

If we divide the **product** (the result of multiplication) of 5 and 7 (which is 35) by either number, we get the other number.

$$35 \div 7 = 5$$
$$35 \div 5 = 7$$

Remember how multiplication is just a shorthand way of showing a lot of addition? You can also think of division as a shorthand way of showing a lot of subtraction. For example, 35 ÷ 7 is the same as asking, "How many times must you subtract 7 from 35 to reach 0?"

$$35 - 7 - 7 - 7 - 7 - 7 = 0$$

That's 5 times!

But what about mixing the order of the numbers up, the way you could with multiplication? This is what a calculator would show.

$$7 \div 35 = 0.2$$
$$5 \div 35 = 0.142857 \ldots$$

Hmm. Those are not the answers we were looking for. Unlike multiplication, the order in which we divide matters. We'll see why in a moment, but first we need to talk about notation.

Notation

Notation is the way you write something. There are some different ways of writing division.

- $9 \div 3$ This is probably the first notation you learned.

- 9/3   This is what your calculator might show.

- $3\overline{)9}$ This sign depicts a long division problem.

- $\dfrac{9}{3}$ This is another common way to show division.

You may have noticed that the last method of showing division looks a lot like a fraction. That's because fractions and division are closely related. Sometimes it is easier to leave a division equation unfinished, because either the answer is hard to write or you hope something else will happen in the equation that will make the division easier. For example, the correct answer to $1 \div 3$ is 0.3333333 …. The dots at the end of the 3s mean that the answer goes on repeating 3 forever. You can never write enough 3s to be exactly correct. So, it's a lot easier to write the answer as the fraction $\dfrac{1}{3}$.

Properties

Unlike multiplication, **division** doesn't have a lot of properties. It's not very flexible. In fact, it's easier to talk about what you *can't* do with division than what you can do.

Order Matters!

Order matters in division. It will give you funny (and wrong!) answers if you change the order of operations. It helps to turn the division equation into plain English so you don't get the order wrong.

Imagine that your teacher wants to divide your class into groups to work on math problems.

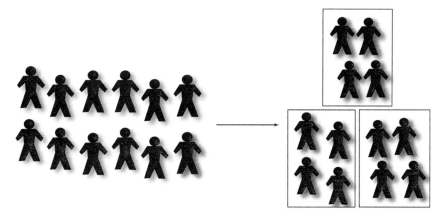

So, you know that there are 12 students in class and the teacher wants 3 groups. How many students will be in each group? We need to divide 12 by 3 to find out.

$$12 \div 3 = 4$$
or
$$12 - 3 - 3 - 3 - 3 = 0$$
We subtracted 3 four times!

In English, the equation is asking, "How many 3s are in the number 12?" If you look at the chart above, you can see that there are 4 groups of 3 in 12. So, your answer is 4.

Notice how the English changes if we change the equation.

$$3 \div 12 = 0.25$$

The equation is now asking, "How many 12s are in the number 3?" Well, because 12 is greater than 3, there isn't even one group of 12 in 3. You'll notice that the subtraction process doesn't work here either. What your calculator tells you when you plug this in is that there is one-quarter of a group of 12 in the number 3 (0.25 is the same as $\frac{1}{4}$).

The different parts of a division equation have different names, because they do different things. We're going to use **variables** to talk about this. You may recall that variables are letters that stand in for numbers when you don't know what the numbers are exactly. A variable could be any number. We will use a, b, and c.

$$a \div b = c$$

or

$$\frac{a}{b} = c$$

a is called the **dividend**: It is the total number you have and want to divide. b is called the **divisor**: It is the number of groups you want to divide the total into; it's the number doing the dividing. c is the **quotient**, the answer or result of division.

Identity Property

$$a \div a = 1$$

or

$$\frac{a}{a} = 1$$

We can prove that these equations are true if we put an example into English. For instance, $3 \div 3$ can be phrased as, "How many groups of 3 are in the number 3?" The answer is 1, because there is exactly 1 group of 3 in the number 3. This also makes sense with the subtraction method; you need to subtract 3 only once from 3 to get to 0.

Division by One

$$a \div 1 = a$$

or

$$\frac{a}{1} = a$$

When we switch the variables for real numbers and turn this into English, this problem asks, "How many ones are in the number seven?" The answer is 7, because you need to subtract one seven times to get to zero.

Division by Zero

$$a \div 0 = \text{no answer}$$

or

$$\frac{a}{0} = \text{no answer}$$

When you divide by 0 on your calculator, it probably says "error." Some might say "infinity." This is because dividing by 0 is undefined—it's not so much a number as it is a placeholder waiting for a number to step in.

Let's think about $2 \div 0$ as a subtraction problem.

$$2 - 0 - 0 - 0 - 0 \dots$$

You can see that you'll never get to 0, no matter how many 0s you subtract from 2. Therefore, we say that division by 0 has no meaning. It's undefined. In English, we can ask, "How many groups of 0 are in 2?" This is like asking, "How much nothing is in something?" That's a hard question to answer! If you ever divide by 0 on a test, you should go back and check your work, because you have probably made a mistake.

Distributive Property

$$\frac{(a+b)}{c} = \frac{a}{c} + \frac{b}{c}$$

When you combine addition or subtraction with division, there are times when you can distribute, or spread, the multiplication operation over the numbers being added. This is called the **distributive property** of division. We can plug in some real numbers to prove it.

$$\frac{(2+4)}{2} = \frac{6}{2} = 3$$

$$\frac{(2+4)}{2} = \frac{2}{2} + \frac{4}{2} = 1 + 2 = 3$$

Negative numbers

Division by negative numbers requires some memorization. When you divide a positive by a positive, you get a positive answer. When you divide a negative by a negative, you get a positive answer. When the signs are different (such as a negative divided by a positive) you get a negative answer. The following table shows this relationship:

$$\text{positive} \div \text{positive} = \text{positive}$$
$$\text{positive} \div \text{negative} = \text{negative}$$
$$\text{negative} \div \text{negative} = \text{positive}$$

You can think about it this way: When a negative and a positive are divided, there is nothing to cancel out the negative, so it must remain in the answer. When two negatives are divided, their negative signs cancel out. If it helps, you can think of the negative sign as dividing by a −1, and you can do anything to it that you would to a normal 1.

ONE MORE THING... Division is a quick way of showing lots of subtraction. It can also help you check your math. If you have just multiplied something and you think you have a questionable answer, you can divide the product by one of the original numbers and see if you get the other original number. If you do, then your answer is correct!

# Participate

Activity: Hands-On

Walk around your house or neighborhood and divide everything you see. In the kitchen, is there a stack of 8 dinner plates? Divide those by 2 and count up the stack with your fingers—1, 2, 3, 4 as one group, 1, 2, 3, 4 as other group. Outside, do you see 5 steps on your front stoop? Divide by 2, as best you can! Are there traffic lights on your street that can be counted and divided? Seek opportunities to divide numbers of things for fun in everyday life!

In a Nutshell

Definitions

- **Division:** a shorthand way of showing a lot of subtraction

- $\dfrac{a}{b} = c$: a is the dividend, b is the divisor, and c is the quotient

Rules

- $a \div 1 = a$

- $a \div 0 =$ undefined, or no answer

- $a \div b \neq b \div a$

- $\dfrac{(a+b)}{c} = \dfrac{a}{c} + \dfrac{b}{c}$

Answers for Opening Page:

There are 372 nickels in the jar.

 Answers for Dive Right In:

1. $79. Whether students round the individual numbers or add them all up and then round, they should still get $79. If students get $81, they rounded drinks to $2.

2. $78.60

3. $6.29. This answer is based on the $78.60 and is rounded up from $6.288.

4. $78.60 + $6.29 = $84.89

5. $84.89(.15) = $12.7335, which rounds to $12.73

6. $84.89 + $12.73 = $97.62

7. $24.41. Remember, the 4 adults are contributing! So divide the total by 4 and you get $24.41.

Fractions and Ratios

A **fraction** shows us the relationship between a whole and a part of that whole. For instance, a whole pizza is made of 8 slices. If you eat one slice, then only a fraction of the original pizza will remain on the table—seven slices out of eight. We can write this as a fraction.

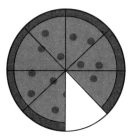

$$\frac{Slices\ Left}{Slices\ Total} = \frac{Part}{Whole} = \frac{7}{8}$$

Pizza minus one slice

At the end of this lesson, you will be able to:

- create and read fractions and ratios

- reduce larger fractions into smaller fractions

Parent's Corner

Invite your fifth grader to see fractions in everyday life. If you split a pizza, ask them how much of the pizza they'd like. $\frac{1}{8}$? $\frac{1}{4}$? $\frac{1}{2}$? Additionally, help your students understand the important difference between fractions and ratios. While fractions represent a part out of the whole, ratios represent a part in relation to another *part*. A fraction of $\frac{3}{4}$ implies that the whole is four parts, and we've taken up three of those parts. A 3:4 ratio implies that the whole is seven parts (3 + 4) and that there are three parts for every four parts. Keep drilling this distinction with your student.

Dive Right In!

Survey Your Friends

Directions: Select your favorite color out of the choices below and share your answers with a group of your friends. Record everyone's answers in the chart below and then answer the questions.

Favorite Color	Red	Orange	Yellow	Green	Blue	Purple
People Who Picked It						

1. How many people are in your group of friends?

2. What fraction of people chose blue?

3. What fraction of people chose red or green?

4. What fraction of people did NOT choose the most popular color?

5. What is the ratio of purple to orange?

6. What is the ratio of the most popular color to the least popular color?

Answers can be found on page 206.

Explore

Parts of a Fraction

These are the parts of a fraction:

$$\frac{part}{whole} = \frac{numerator}{denominator} = \frac{10}{2}$$

The number on the top of the fraction is called the **numerator**. The number on the bottom, the one doing the dividing, is called the **denominator** or the **divisor**. We'll be using these terms in this and the next few chapters.

You're probably familiar with the fraction $\frac{1}{3}$. It shows that the number 1 is being divided by the number 3. But it also shows that the 1 is part of a whole of 3.

Specifically, it's one-third. Let's take a closer look.

Whole pepperoni pizza $\frac{1}{1}$

That's a whole pepperoni pizza. You might want to take a slice, but you can't, because no one has sliced it into pieces yet. There is 1 whole pizza, and it's divided into 1 piece. Therefore, we have $\frac{1}{1}$ of a pizza. That's not too useful, so let's cut it up.

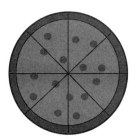

Pizza divided $\quad\frac{8}{8}$
into eight pieces

That's better. Like most pizzas, ours has 8 slices. We have 1 whole pizza divided into 8 parts. No one has eaten any slices yet, so all 8 pieces are on the table. So, we have $\frac{8}{8}$ ("eight-eighths") of a pizza. Why is that 8 on the bottom? That's how many slices make up the whole pizza now. The 8 is on the top because that's how many parts of the pizza we still have. Dig in!

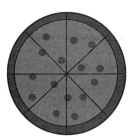

Pizza divided $\quad\frac{8}{8}$
into eight pieces

Now you've taken a slice and eaten it. Let's take stock: We have 7 slices of the pizza out of a whole 8. In other words,

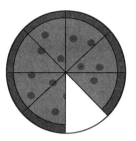

Pizza minus one slice

$$\frac{part}{whole} = \frac{Slices\ Left}{Slices\ In\ Total} = \frac{7}{8}$$

If you ate another piece, then we would have $\frac{6}{8}$ of a pizza left.

Equivalent Fractions

Hold on a second! If we have $\frac{6}{8}$ of a pizza left, that means you have eaten $\frac{2}{8}$ of a pizza, right? You might not have thought of it that way. Compare the following two pictures of the pizza.

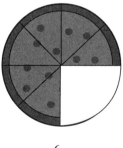

$\frac{6}{8}$ of pizza

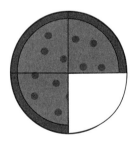

$\frac{3}{4}$ of pizza

The pizza on the left was divided into 8 slices. The pizza on the right was cut into 4 slices. But you can see that the same amount is missing from each whole, no matter how it was sliced. This is because $\frac{6}{8}$ and $\frac{3}{4}$ are **equivalent fractions**—they are different ways of showing the same relationship. We obtained this equivalent fraction by **reducing** $\frac{6}{8}$ to $\frac{3}{4}$.

To reduce a fraction, you divide the numerator and denominator by the same number. If both numbers in the fraction are even, start by dividing by 2. If they are not even, try small odd numbers like 3 and 5. Let's reduce $\frac{6}{8}$.

$$\frac{6 \div 2}{8 \div 2} = \frac{3}{4}$$

Let's see how we can simplify another.

$$\frac{56 \div 2}{100 \div 2} = \frac{28}{50} \rightarrow \frac{28 \div 2}{50 \div 2} = \frac{14}{25}$$

That's as far as we can simplify it. You might have noticed that we could have divided the top and bottom by 4 instead of dividing by 2 twice. It might have saved us some time, but both methods get us to the right answer.

Ratios

Ratios show the relationship between two different parts of a whole. Be careful not to confuse ratios with fractions, which compare one part to the whole. They may look similar, but here's the difference:

$$fraction = \frac{part}{whole}$$

$$ratio = \frac{part}{part}$$

A ratio can also be represented with a colon, like $x{:}y$. Let's say that there are 50 girls and 60 boys at the school dance. The ratio of girls to boys is 50:60. Notice that the ratio of boys to girls is the reverse, 60:50.

If we want, we can reduce this ratio like a fraction. Dividing each side by 10, we see that the ratio is 5:6, girls to boys. For every 5 girls, there are 6 boys. Sometimes people will talk about this reduced number by dividing it even further: (5 girls) ÷ (6 boys) = 0.83 girls per boy. This last division is useful; it's like saying that the ratio is 0.83:1. It sets the ratio in terms of one boy. How would you write it so that the ratio is in terms of one girl?

ONE MORE THING... We live in a world filled with fractions. Newspapers are filled with statistics, such as "nearly two-thirds of people polled support the mayor." When people talk about decimals or percents, they are talking about fractions. When you ask for a half of a glass of water, you are using fractions.

Ratios are also used a lot. They allow us to show the relationship between the different numbers in our lives. For example, the ratio of students to teachers is used to advertise the amount of personal attention each student receives at a particular school.

Participate

Activity: Hands-On

Gather a few note cards and some pens or pencils. Put the notecards on the floor and write a number on each card—any number at all. One card could be "1" and another could be "1349." Make a few of these—10–12 total. Be sure to make a few nice, round, even numbers like 100, 80, 4. Also, have one card be the dividing line. So, for example

Move the number cards around and look at the different fractions you make. Try to reduce them. Point to the card that is the denominator. Point to the card that is the numerator. See if you have any equivalent fractions in the bunch.

In a Nutshell

Definitions

- **Fraction:** a way of showing the relationship of a part to a whole, often written as $\dfrac{part}{whole}$

- **Numerator:** the number on top of the fraction

- **Denominator:** the number on the bottom of the fraction, also called the divisor

- **Equivalent Fractions:** fractions that show the same proportion with different numbers, such as $\dfrac{5}{10}$ and $\dfrac{1}{2}$

- **Reducing:** simplifying a fraction to its smallest equivalent; for instance, $\dfrac{5}{15}$ reduces to $\dfrac{1}{3}$

- **Ratio:** a relationship between two parts in a whole, often written as $\dfrac{part}{part}$

Answers for Dive Right In:

Answers will vary, as the numbers depend on the responses by the child.

By way of example, if the ratio were 3:4:5:2:3:6 for R, O, Y, G, B, & P, respectively, the answers to the questions would be as follows:

1. 23

2. $\dfrac{3}{23}$

3. $R + G = 3 + 3 = \dfrac{6}{23}$

4. In this case, Purple was the most popular. $\dfrac{17}{23}$ did NOT pick Purple (because 6 did).

5. P:O = 6:4 = 3:2. Remind students that the first color mentioned has to be the first color in the ratio.

6. Purple was most popular at 6. Green was the least popular at 2.
So P:G = 6:2 = 3:1.

Adding and Subtracting Fractions

You'll be asked to add and subtract fractions a lot in life, as well as on many test types. Imagine you have a recipe for salad dressing that asks you to add the ingredients into a jar—you've only got one jar, and you need to know that all the stuff is going to fit into it. If the jar holds 2 cups, can you fit it in all the ingredients? Here are your ingredients.

$\dfrac{1}{4}$ cup sour cream; $\dfrac{1}{3}$ cup vinegar; $1\dfrac{1}{2}$ cups extra virgin olive oil

Seems like a tight fit. We'll need to add the different parts together to see if we can get them all in there.

$$\frac{1}{4}+\frac{1}{3}+1\frac{1}{2}=?$$

All the ingredients add up to $2\dfrac{7}{18}$, too big for a 2-cup jar.

At the end of this lesson, you will be able to:

- use the Bowtie Method to add and subtract fractions
- use the Bowtie Method to compare the relative sizes of fractions

---

Parent's Corner

Adding and subtracting fractions—particularly fractions with different denominators—is one of trickiest math concepts for students of this age (and many ages, frankly)! In later grades, students will have access to a calculator to solve these questions for them, but it is crucial that they take the time to add and subtract fractions *by hand* in grade 5. Resist at all costs the urge to simply use a calculator!

Dive Right In!

Musical Fractions

Directions: Musicians use fractions when composing and reading music. Study this information and answer the questions.

These are whole notes:

These are half notes. Half notes are half as long as a whole note.

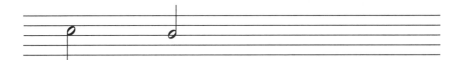

These are quarter notes. Quarter notes are half as long as a half note and a quarter as long as a whole note.

These are eighth notes.

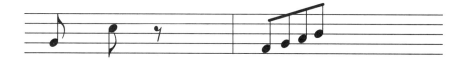

Use the previous information to answer these questions.

1. Eighth notes are as long as a quarter note.

2. Eighth notes are as long as a half note.

3. Eighth notes are as long as a whole note.

To summarize:

Notes (in decreasing length)

| 1 | 1/2 | 1/4 | 1/8 |

Musicians also use fractions when reading time signatures. A time signature is the fraction that appears at the beginning of a line of music. The top number represents the number of notes per measure, or bar of music. The bottom number represents the type of note. So, for example, 3/4 would mean that a measure contains three (3) quarter notes (4).

4. In this example, what is the time signature?

5. Translate the time signature into words.

There are three errors in note length in the below music. Circle them and write in the correct notes.

Answers can be found on page 216.

Explore

How to Add Fractions

Can we just add up the numerators and denominators to add fractions? Nope. A little thought experiment shows us why: Half a pizza plus half a pizza makes a whole pizza, right? So, if we add the numerators and the denominators of $\frac{1}{2} + \frac{1}{2}$ we should get 1, correct? Well, if we add up numerators and denominators, we get $\frac{2}{4}$, or one half, which is wrong. Two halves don't make another half! We should have gotten a whole pizza, $\frac{2}{2}$, when we added two half-pizzas. So, *never add denominators*. First, make the denominators the same and then add all the numerators.

Bowtie Addition

We know how to add fractions when the denominators are the same—just add the numerators and keep the same denominator.

$$\frac{3}{5} + \frac{3}{5} = \frac{6}{5} = 1\frac{1}{5}$$

What about when the denominators are different? That's where the **Bowtie Method** comes in. Take a look at this diagram.

Problem	Bowtie	Answer
$\frac{a}{b} + \frac{c}{d}$	$\frac{a}{b} \diagdown\kern-0.6em\diagup \frac{c}{d}$ $ad+bc$	$\frac{ad+bc}{bd}$

Everywhere you see an arrow, *multiply* in the direction of the arrow and write the answer. Let's add $\frac{2}{5}+\frac{1}{3}$ using this technique.

First, multiply the denominators.

$$\frac{2}{5}+\frac{1}{3}=\frac{}{5\times 3}=\frac{}{15}$$

Now, multiply diagonally and add the results to find the new numerator.

$$\overset{2\times 3\ +\ 5\times 1}{\frac{2}{5}\times\frac{1}{3}}=\frac{}{15}$$

$$\overset{6\ +\ 5}{\frac{2}{5}\ +\ \frac{1}{3}}=\frac{11}{15}$$

It works every time!

Bowtie Subtraction

You can use the bowtie method on subtraction problems too. You just have to make sure that you keep your numbers in order. Otherwise, you will get the wrong answer.

$$\frac{8}{9}-\frac{2}{5}=\frac{40-18}{45}=\frac{22}{45}$$

$$\frac{8}{9}-\frac{2}{5}=\frac{18-40}{45}=-\frac{22}{45}$$

Comparing Fractions

The Bowtie Method can also be used to compare fractions quickly. For example, in a pie-eating contest, Jack ate $\frac{3}{4}$ of a pie and Jill ate $\frac{5}{7}$. Who ate more?

$$21\quad \frac{3}{4}\times\frac{5}{7}\quad 20$$

You don't need to multiply across the bottom when comparing. Just multiply diagonally, and the fraction with the bigger number next to it is the greater one. It looks like Jack won!

There are lots of opportunities to add and subtract fractions in life. When you get change for a dollar, you are dealing in fractions. Basically, any job that involves money requires a solid knowledge of fractions. Cooking and construction work also require addition and subtraction of fractions all the time. You can also use fractions to understand and read music.

Participate

Activity 1: Hands-On

Add with a "Fraction Pie." Draw a Pie on paper and then cut it into equal slices. Remove some of the Pie and write a fraction that shows the amount you have taken away from the whole pie. Then, remove another part of the pie and write a fraction to show that amount. Add the two amounts. Write down the fraction of the pie that is left after you remove the two amounts. Finally, replace the slices to make it whole again.

Activity 2: Hands-On

Look up sheet music online or in a book. Based on the what you have learned about half notes, quarter notes, full notes, go from left to right down the line identifying the length of each note. Say out loud what type of note each is.

Using the note cards from the previous exercise, add and subtract fractions on the floor, remembering the rules we covered in the Bowtie methods.

In a Nutshell

Rules

- How to add fractions with the Bowtie Method:

$$
\begin{array}{ccc}
\text{Problem} & \text{Bowtie} & \text{Answer} \\[4pt]
 & ad + bc & \\
\dfrac{a}{b} + \dfrac{c}{d} & \dfrac{a}{b}\!\times\!\dfrac{c}{d} & \dfrac{ad + bc}{bd}
\end{array}
$$

- When you subtract fractions, just replace the plus sign (+) with a minus sign (−) and keep the numbers in order.

Answers for Dive Right In:

1. They are half as long (you have to divide by two to get from 1/4 to 1/8).

2. They are 1/4 as long.

3. They are 1/8 as long. There are eight eighth notes in a whole note.

4. There are four quarter notes in a measure and the numbers say 4 and 4. So the answer is 4/4 because there are 4 notes in a measure and each note is a quarter note.

5. There are 4 quarter notes in each measure.

Multiplying and Dividing Fractions

Y ou'll be asked to multiply and divide fractions a lot in life, as well as in school and on many test types. Imagine that you are baking a cake and the recipe says it will serve 8 people. You only need to serve 4 people, so you want to cut the recipe in half.

Instead of using 6 eggs, you will use 3; instead of using 1 cup of milk, you will use a half cup of milk; and so on. But what do you do with that $\frac{1}{4}$ cup of sugar? What's half of a quarter?

Half of a quarter is $\frac{1}{8}$.

At the end of this lesson, you will be able to:

- multiply and divide fractions
- use canceling to simplify fractions in equations

Parent's Corner

With mastery of multiplying and dividing fractions, fifth graders begin to have total fluency with fractions. They can add, subtract, multiply, and divide them! Make sure, though, that your student understands the different approach to adding and subtracting fractions as opposed to multiplying and dividing. Moreover, do they understand that when we divide fractions we are merely multiplying by the reciprocal?

Dive Right In!

Statistics and Fractions

Directions: We often hear on television that "4 out of 5 dentists recommend ..." or "7 out of 10 people polled said that ...." One way of understanding these numbers, or statistics, is with fractions and ratios. Fractions and ratios are usually created by asking a lot of people questions and simplifying the results. Answer the following questions.

1. If 4 out of 5 dentists recommend a particular toothpaste, and 2,000 dentists were polled, how many dentists DO NOT support that toothpaste?

2. If there are 8 million people in New York City, and 1 out of 40 Americans is a millionaire, how many millionaires should there be in New York City?

3. If 1 out of every 1,000 people in the United States is named Harold, and there are 300 million people in the United States, how many Harolds are there?

Answers can be found on page 224.

Explore

Fraction Multiplication

How do you figure out what $\dfrac{3}{5}$ of \$20 is? We can draw it out.

The whole thing is worth 20	Cut into 5 equal pieces	So each piece is worth 4	Count 3 of them
		4	4
		4	4
		4	4
		4	4
		4	4

But what if we don't have time to draw the picture? This problem asks us to multiply fractions. If one of the numbers we are multiplying by is an integer, we can put it over 1 to make it a fraction. As an equation, $\dfrac{3}{5}$ of 20 can be written as

$$\frac{3}{5} \times \frac{20}{1} =$$

We just multiply straight across the top and straight across the bottom. Unlike addition, we don't have to start or end with the same denominator.

$$\frac{3}{5} \times \frac{20}{1} = \frac{3 \times 20}{5 \times 1} = \frac{60}{5} = 12$$

So, multiplying fractions is actually simpler than adding or subtracting them. You just multiply straight across.

$$\frac{a}{b} \times \frac{c}{d} = \frac{ac}{bd}$$

Canceling

Canceling, like reducing, helps us simplify our math. It's a great tool! Take $\dfrac{2}{3} \times \dfrac{21}{4}$, for example. Before we multiply straight across, we look to see if *any* of the numbers on top have a common factor with *any* of the numbers on the bottom. If so, divide both numbers by the factor and cancel. For instance, the numbers 2 and 4 have "2" as a common factor. The numbers 3 and 21 have "3" as a common factor. Let's divide the numbers by their common factors.

$$\frac{2}{3} \times \frac{21}{4}$$

$$\frac{2}{3} \times \frac{21}{4}$$

$$\frac{2}{3} \times \frac{21}{4}$$

$$\frac{\overset{1}{2}}{3} \times \frac{21}{\underset{2}{4}}$$

$$\frac{\overset{1}{2}}{\underset{1}{3}} \times \frac{\overset{7}{21}}{\underset{2}{4}}$$

$$\frac{1}{1} \times \frac{7}{2}$$

$$\boxed{\frac{7}{2}}$$

That should be faster!

Fraction Division

Dividing fractions is a lot like multiplying fractions. It has only one more step. Remember: *When dividing, don't ask why, flip the second and multiply.*

What is $\dfrac{3}{4} \div \dfrac{5}{7}$?

Let's flip (or take the reciprocal of) the second fraction and multiply straight across the top and bottom.

$$\frac{3}{4} \div \frac{5}{7} = \frac{3}{4} \times \frac{7}{5} = \frac{21}{20}$$

Just remember: Don't cancel until *after* the flip!

ONE MORE THING... The same jobs that require you to know how to add and subtract fractions require you to know how to multiply and divide them. Multiplying and dividing fractions are staples of science, finance, cooking, construction, music, and many other jobs that might surprise you.

 **Participate**

Activity: Hands-On

You will need a few things for this activity: note cards (or small squares of paper) and a pen. Write numbers on the pieces of paper and then, using what you learned in the chapter, practice fraction multiplication and division (including canceling) with the cards.

In a Nutshell

Definition

- **Canceling:** a method of simplifying multiplication and division of fractions

Hints

- **Multiplying fractions** is simple; just multiply straight across.

- **Dividing fractions** is similar; flip a fraction and multiply across.

Answers for Dive Right In:

1. If 4 out of 5 dentists recommend a toothpaste, then 1 out of 5 don't. 1 out of 5 is 400 out of 2,000. Students can also find 4 out of 5, which is 1,600 and subtract from 2,000 to find the answer.

2. It's all about the ratios: 200,000.

3. 300,000.

Translating English into Math

In word problems, you see lots of words but hardly any numbers. But by identifying certain code words and phrases, you can turn a word problem into a math problem!

At the end of this lesson, you will be able to:

- identify the code words and phrases in a word problem

- translate those words and phrases into math problems

Parent's Corner

Fifth graders *loathe* word problems! They are no fun at all. When we translate English into math, we can help make word problems a lot less daunting. Remind them that every word problem is simply asking you to apply the fundamental skills you *already know* (addition, subtraction, multiplication, division, etc.) in a context you may not have seen before.

Dive Right In!

Survey

Directions: Read the below information, translate it, and use it to answer the question.

For a class project, you decide to poll your peers about their use of technology. Here is the data.

Out of the 214 students in your class, 132 complete your survey.

Of those who completed the survey, you learn the following: Half the students have portable audio devices, 112 have cell phones, and 25% do not have home computers. Everyone who has a portable audio device also has a cell phone. Everyone who has a home computer has a cell phone.

1. What is the ratio of students surveyed who have portable audio devices to students who have computers?

2. What percent of students surveyed do NOT have cell phones?

3.   How many students surveyed do NOT have portable audio devices?

4.   How many students surveyed have home computers?

5.   What percent of students completed the survey?

Answers can be found on page 235.

Explore

Understanding the English

Look at problems 1 and 2. Which one's easier to do?

1. What is one-fourth of the difference between forty percent of 110 and twenty percent of 80?

2. $\dfrac{1}{4} \times (44 - 16) =$

Problem 2 is a little more straightforward: It looks like math. Problem 1 hardly looks like math. There are lots of words but only a few numbers, and it's unclear what you're supposed to do with those words and numbers. Knowing how to translate words into math can help you make problems like the first one look more like the second one.

Sometimes questions will be purposely confusing. Be careful when you see problems like this one.

⇨ Helena is half as old as Mariana, who is one-third her Aunt Gertrude's age. If Helena is 10, how old is Aunt Gertrude?

First, keep track of each person's relationship. Mariana is one-third Aunt Gertrude's age and Helena is half as old as Mariana. It's easy to get confused with these types of questions, so pay extra attention when you see things like this.

Let's say the question said the following instead.

⇨ Helena is half as old as Mariana and one-third her Aunt Gertrude's age. If Helena is 10, how old is Aunt Gertrude?

Then it would be *Helena* who is one-third of Aunt Gertrude's age. Be careful of the words *which* and *who* and *that*—make sure you understand the relationship that's being described.

Here is a math translation of some of the most common words and phrases you'll see in word problems.

- *What* or *how much* or *what is the value of*—the part that actually asks you a particular amount or value—can be translated as *x* or any other variable.
- *Of*—as in *25% of* or *one-fifth of*—means you are multiplying.
- *Fraction of* or *part of* means you're finding a fraction, or putting one number over another.
- *Is, are,* or *equals* means "=."
- *Product* is what you get when you multiply.
- *Quotient* is what you get when you divide.
- *Sum, total, more than,* or *all together* means you're adding.
- *Difference* or *less than* means you're subtracting.
- *Percent* means divide by 100.

Translating Percents

Try translating the following word problems into math:

1.   What is eight percent of three hundred?

2.   What is one-sixth of eight percent of three hundred?

3.   What is four times one-sixth of eight percent of three hundred?

4.   48 is what percent of 120?

In the first few problems, you were given a specific percent, so you didn't have to worry about translating. However, when you see *what percent*, translate it as $\dfrac{x}{100}$, because any percent is really just that number over 100. For example,

$$4\% = \dfrac{4}{100} \qquad 17\% = \dfrac{17}{100} \qquad 300\% = \dfrac{300}{100} \qquad 1{,}000\% = \dfrac{1{,}000}{100} \qquad 0.1\% = \dfrac{0.1}{100}$$

$$\dfrac{1}{2}\% = \dfrac{\frac{1}{2}}{100}$$

Let's look back at question 4 on the last page: 48 is what percent of 120? Translate and solve.

Now try these. Translate and solve.

5.   48 is what percent of 80 percent of 120?

6. $\dfrac{1}{2}$ of 48 is what percent of 80 percent of 120?

Translating Fractions

This one's a little different.

    1.   The square root of 49 is what fraction of 28?

The square root part is pretty clear; that's $\sqrt{49}$, or 7.

When you see a question asking "x is what fraction of y?" you put the x over y in a fraction and then reduce if possible. If we rewrite the question with 7 in place of "The square root of 49," it now asks, "7 is what fraction of 28?" Well, 7 is the x and 28 is the y.

$$\frac{7}{28} =$$

Reduce and that's your answer.

Try some more.

    2.   5 is what fraction of 25? _____

You may also see it phrased this way:

    3.   120 is what part of 480? _____

Let's combine some of these terms.

    4.   The square root of 144 is what percent of one-fourth of 240? _____

Just take it step by step, one phrase at a time.

Word Problems

Thought you were already doing word problems? You were, but some word problems have even more words and a whole story.

    1.   Let's say you're a real estate agent and you sold thirty houses during the first three months of this year. This number is 120% of the number of houses you sold during the same period last year. How many houses did you sell during the first three months last year?

Pick out the important information, which is usually near the numbers.

You sold 30 houses. That's 120% more than last year.

You really don't need the rest of the words.

Now translate, thinking "30 is 120% of what number?"

2.   At the beginning of 2005, Jeanine had $900 in her bank account. She earns 5% interest, compounded every 6 months. If Jeanine makes no more deposits, how much will she have in the account at the end of 2005?

Answers can be found on page 235.

 You don't always see a straightforward math problem with just numbers and operational symbols (−, ×, ÷, +). You need to translate English words into math so you can see what the question is asking.

Banks don't give you equations to figure out how much money you earn on your savings account. Nor do stores give you equations to figure out how much you can save on those sale items. They explain the problem in English and leave you to figure out the rest.

Participate

Activity: Hands-On

Search for math or math problems in everyday life. Look at some recipes and see the fractions and numbers. Read an article (online or newspaper or magazine) and watch for math language or mathematical problems within those. Specifically, look for numbers or mathematical phrases that can be translated: Does the article refer to $\frac{1}{2}$ of the residents of a town voting for something? Or $\frac{2}{3}$ of mothers agreeing on a preferred peanut butter brand? Or a 120% increase in school enrollments?

In a Nutshell

Hints

- Focus on the code words in the word problem and ignore the unimportant words.

- Write out your equation piece by piece—each code word should have a place in the equation.

- Here are the most common code words and their translations.

    - *What* or *how much* or *what is the value of*—the part that actually asks you a particular amount or value—can be translated as *x* or any other variable.

    - *Of*—as in *25 percent of* or *one-fifth of*—means you are multiplying.

    - *Fraction of* or *part of* means you're finding a fraction, or putting one number over another.

    - *Is*, *are*, or *equals* means "=."

    - *Product* is what you get when you multiply.

    - *Quotient* is what you get when you divide.

    - *Sum*, *total*, *more than*, or *all together* means you're adding.

    - *Difference* or *less than* means you're subtracting.

    - *Percent* means divide by 100.

Answers for Dive Right In:

1. 2:3
2. 15%
3. 66
4. 99
5. 62%

 Answers for Explore:

Understanding the English

1st Arrow: Aunt Gertrude is 60.

2nd Arrow: Aunt Gertrude is 30.

Translating Percents

1. $x = \dfrac{8}{100} \times 300$ $(x = 24)$

2. $x = \dfrac{1}{6} \times \dfrac{8}{100} \times 300$ $(x = 4)$

3. $x = 4 \times \dfrac{1}{6} \times \dfrac{8}{100} \times 300$

$(x = 16)$

4. $48 = \dfrac{x}{100} \times 120$ $(x = 40)$

5. $48 = \dfrac{x}{100} \times 120$

$(x = 50,$ so it's 50%)

6. $\dfrac{1}{2} \times 48 = \dfrac{x}{100} \times \dfrac{80}{100} \times 120$

$(x = 25,$ so that's 25%)

Translating Fractions

1. $\dfrac{1}{4}$

2. $\dfrac{1}{5}$

3. $\dfrac{1}{4}$

4. $12 = \dfrac{x}{100} \times \dfrac{1}{4} \times 240$

$(x = 20,$ so that's 20%)

Translating Exponents & Roots

1. $x = 3$

2. $\sqrt{100 - 36} = \dfrac{50}{100} x$ $(x = 16)$

3. $x^3 = 2x^2$ $(x = 2)$

4. $\dfrac{200}{100} x = \dfrac{600}{100} \times 6$ $(x = 18)$

Word Problems

1. 25
2. $992.25

Decimals

Decimals are very similar to fractions. You can recognize a decimal by its **decimal point**, the little period in the number. A decimal is another way to represent part of a whole. Everything written to the right of the decimal point represents a number less than 1.

Think about money. One dollar can be broken into cents, right? But let's say you still want to represent it as a dollar. Would you write, "I have a dollar and a $\frac{1}{4}$"? No, you would write, "I have $0.25." The decimal .25 represents a quarter, which is also one-fourth of a dollar.

At the end of this lesson, you will be able to:

- translate from fractions to decimals and from decimals to fractions
- compare decimals to find the largest one
- perform basic algebra with decimals

Parent's Corner

Once fifth graders learn about decimals, they will see them everywhere! Show them decimals on receipts or bills and challenge them to add or subtract the decimals. Encourage them to read decimals out loud as well. (e.g., "Four and 7 tenths" or "Nine and 18 hundredths."). This will help reinforce the concept of decimal places.

Dive Right In!

Food Shopping

Directions: You have $150 to buy groceries for the next 14 days. Sales tax on food is 8%. You are a very organized person and a creature of habit. For breakfast, you always eat 2 eggs and a container of yogurt. For lunch, you always eat a sandwich made with 6 ounces of tuna fish, an apple, and a bottle of iced tea. For dinner, you microwave a frozen dinner and have an ice cream bar for dessert.

Here are your local supermarket's prices. Fill in the chart. You can buy food that will last more than 14 days, but the groceries must last at least 14 days.

Grocery Item	Quantity in Package	Cost per Package	# Packages Needed for 14 Days	Cost for Number of Packages Purchased	Sales Tax for Total	Total Cost of Item
Eggs	12 eggs	$1.99				
Yogurt	6 containers	$3.19				
Bread	26 slices	$2.89				
Tuna	6 ounces	$0.89				
Apples	1 apple	$0.99				
Iced Tea	12 bottles	$9.99				

Grocery Item	Quantity in Package	Cost per Package	# Packages Needed for 14 Days	Cost for Number of Packages Purchased	Sales Tax for Total	Total Cost of Item
Frozen Dinners	1 box	$4.29				
Ice Cream Bars	8 bars	$3.49				
					Grand Total	

Use the information in the chart to answer the questions on the next page.

1. Do you have enough money to pay for all the groceries?

2. If you don't have enough, how much more do you need?

3. If you have extra, how much extra do you have?

Answers can be found on page 249.

 **Explore**

Reading and Writing Decimals

For whole numbers (0, 1, 2, 3, and so on) that are divided into 10, 100, 1,000, or more parts.

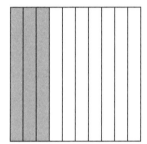

The square above is divided into ten equal parts. Three parts are shaded. From your fractions chapter, you know that this means $\frac{3}{10}$ are shaded. This can be written as 0.3.

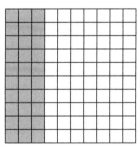

Now let's take the square above and divide those 10 parts by 10 parts. You now have 100 equal parts, and now 30 parts are shaded. This can be written as $\frac{30}{100}$, or 0.30. Since the same amount of the square is shaded, the decimals 0.3 and 0.30 are equal. Adding 0s to the right of a decimal does not change the number. In other words, 0.3 = 0.30 = 0.300 = 0.3000, and so on.

Fractions in the Decimal Places

Just as the places to the left of the decimal point have place-value names, so do the places to the right of the decimal. So when you're talking about a quarter, or $.25, the 2 and the 5 each have a specific place value.

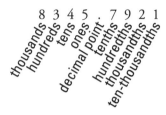

Let's talk about the relationship between fractions and decimal places. The place to the right of the decimal point is called the **tenths** place. This means that whatever number falls in this spot can be written as a fraction with 10 as the denominator.

1. Because 7 is in the tenths place, how could you write it as a fraction?

To the right of the tenths place, we have the **hundredths** place—named because you can take the two-digit number to the right of the decimal and place it over 100 to turn it into a fraction.

2. How would you write 9 hundredths as a fraction?

3. How about this one: If you wanted to write 9 hundredths as a decimal, how would you write it?

4. Based on what we've learned so far, how do you think the **thousandths** place gets its name?

5. How would you represent the 2 in the number on the previous page as a fraction?

6. How would you write the 1 in the number on the previous page as a fraction?

Remember how the value of the places gets smaller as you go from left to right? This continues to the right of the decimal point as well. One-thousandth is smaller than one-hundredth, which is smaller than one-tenth.

Repeating Decimals

When you have a decimal with a line over it, the digits that are under the line repeat forever to the right.

Here are some examples:

$3.7\overline{52}$ means that this number is actually 3.752525252 …

$1.\overline{6}$ means that this number is actually 1.66666 …. Notice that this number can also be written as $1.6\overline{6}$ or $1.66\overline{6}$. These are all the same number.

Comparing Decimals

Now that we've talked about what decimals are, let's talk about comparing decimals and numbers with decimals. The first step is to align the decimal points so that the same place values are sitting on top of each other.

Compare 2.1341 and 2.153.

First stack the numbers,

$$2.1341$$
$$2.153$$

Then look at the numbers in each place. Working from left to right, compare the digits in each set until you find the place where the digits aren't equal. Start with the biggest place, which in this case is the *ones* or *units* place.

$$2.1341$$
$$2.153$$

Both numbers have a 2 in the ones place. So let's move on to the *tenths* place.

2.**1**341
2.**1**53

1 is in the tenths place for both numbers. Now look at the *hundredths*:

2.1**3**41
2.1**5**3

These two digits are different. Because 5 is bigger than 3, 2.153 is greater than 2.1341. Notice that it doesn't matter that 2.1341 has more digits; what matters is the values of the digits in the same places.

Turning Decimals into Fractions

Let's talk about how to turn any decimal into a fraction. We'll start with an example.

0.2

The 2 is in the tenths place, so you would write it as $\dfrac{2}{10}$. Now simplify it. Both numbers are divisible by 2, so you can reduce the fraction to $\dfrac{1}{5}$. In other words, 0.2 can be rewritten as $\dfrac{1}{5}$.

If you want to turn a decimal into a fraction, find the digit that's the farthest to the right and put the number over the appropriate denominator for that placeholder. For instance, if the decimal goes out to the hundredths place, turn it into a fraction by putting those two digits over 100.

Let's try a more difficult decimal.

0.425

The 5 is the digit that's farthest to the right. It's in the thousandths place. So put the entire number over 1,000: $\dfrac{425}{1,000}$. Again, let's try to simplify. Both numbers are divisible by 5, which makes the fraction $\dfrac{85}{200}$. You can divide by 5 again to get $\dfrac{17}{40}$. That's as far as this fraction can be reduced, so we're done.

If you have a mixed number, such as 3.8, keep the whole number the same and change only the decimal. So 3.8 would become $3\frac{8}{10}$, which reduces to $3\frac{4}{5}$.

Turning Fractions into Decimals

Remember that the fraction bar means "divided by." So $\frac{3}{4}$ means "3 divided by 4." In order to turn decimals into fractions, divide the numerator (top) by the denominator (bottom). The result is the equivalent decimal. Let's turn $\frac{3}{4}$ into a decimal: $4\overline{)3.00}$ with quotient 0.75.

Adding and Subtracting Decimals

To add or subtract decimals, stack the numbers as if you were comparing them. Let's look at the following numbers:

$$32.35$$
$$25.72$$

Now put a decimal below the aligned decimals. This decimal point will *never* move.

$$32.35$$
$$+25.72$$

Now continue to work the problem as if it were a regular addition or subtraction problem, leaving that decimal point exactly where it is.

Let's try adding these three numbers now: 3.2, 7.05, and 4.731.

First, stack them so the decimals line up. Then, put a decimal right under the other decimals, below the equal sign.

$$3.2$$
$$7.05$$
$$+4.731$$
$$.$$

Notice that the numbers don't have the same number of decimal places. Use 0 as a placeholder to fill in empty spaces to the right of the decimal. Remember that adding 0s to the right of the decimal doesn't change the number.

$$\begin{array}{r} 3.200 \\ 7.050 \\ +4.731 \\ \hline \end{array}$$

Now you can add all the columns.

$$\begin{array}{r} 3.200 \\ 7.050 \\ +4.731 \\ \hline 14.981 \end{array}$$

Subtraction works the same way; just change the sign!

Answers can be found on page 250.

Multiplying Decimals

To multiply decimals, start by ignoring the decimal point. Just multiply as if the numbers were integers.

Let's look at the following problem:

$$\begin{array}{r} 4.73 \\ \times 0.06 \\ \hline \end{array}$$

First, multiply and ignore the decimal.

$$\begin{array}{r} 4.73 \\ \times 0.06 \\ \hline 2838 \end{array}$$

Now, add up the number of decimal places in the problem. The first number has 2 and the second number has 2. There is a total of 4 decimal places in the problem. So move the decimal point to the left 4 places in your answer.

$$\begin{array}{r} 4.73 \\ \times 0.06 \\ \hline .2838 \end{array}$$

Dividing Decimals

In order to divide decimals, change the divisor (the number you're dividing by) to an integer by moving the decimal point all the way to the right. When you do this, you *must* move the decimal in the dividend (the number you're dividing into) the same number of places to the right.

Let's look at a problem.

$$0.4\overline{)36.0}$$

In order to make .4 an integer, you must move the decimal one place to the right. Since the decimal in 36 is all the way to the right, in order to move it one more space over, we have to add a 0.

So your new problem is

$$4\overline{)360}$$

Now, solve.

$$4\overline{)360}^{\,90}$$

ONE MORE THING... Decimals can be used anywhere in your life that requires you to express parts of whole numbers.

You've been using decimals for a long time. Every time you pay for something that is not in whole dollars, you and the cashier use decimals.

Decimals are also used in measurements such as length, weight, and height. Scientists frequently use decimals, because they often measure very small amounts of substances.

Participate

Activity 1: Hands-On

Draw a square on your grid with sides that are 10 squares long like below. Make sure the square has a total of 100 squares in it. Draw several 10-by-10 squares. Then, make a different design in each one and color in the design so that 0.33 of each square is colored in. You can also try to color in .75 of each square. See how many different designs you can come up with!

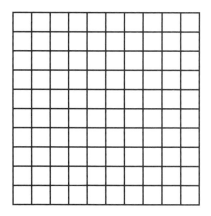

Activity 2: Hands-On

Find a photo in a magazine or newspaper, or even a family photo. The photo should be of a bunch of people all together, in a line, ideally. Pick one person in the middle of the photo to be the "decimal point" and then moving to the left and then moving to the right, identify the place of each other person: tenths, hundredths, thousandths to the right and ones, tens, hundreds and so on, to the left.

In a Nutshell

Definitions

- **Decimals:** a way of representing part of a whole number
- **Decimal Point:** the period inside a number; everything to the right of the decimal point represents a part of a whole number, like the 50 cents in the sum $17.50
- **Tenths:** the first digit to the right of the decimal point is the tenths place, representing fractions of 10
- **Hundredths:** the second digit to the right of the decimal point is the hundredths place, representing fractions of 100
- **Thousandths:** the third digit to the right of the decimal point is the thousandths place, representing fractions of 1,000

Hints

- A bar over part of a decimal, like with $3.7\overline{52}$, means that the numbers under the bar repeat (in this case 3.752525252…).
- When comparing decimals, be sure to compare each decimal place, from left to right.
- When turning decimals into fractions, remember that their last decimal place matters; decimals in the tenths place are fractions of 10, decimals in the hundredths place are fractions of 100, and so on.

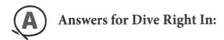

A Answers for Dive Right In:

Grocery Item	Quantity in Package	Cost per Package	# Packages Needed for 14 Days	Cost for Number of Packages Purchased	Sales Tax for Total	Total Cost of Item
Eggs	12 eggs	$1.99	3	$5.97	$0.48	$6.45
Yogurt	6 containers	$3.19	3	$9.57	$0.77	$10.34
Bread	26 slices	$2.89	2	$5.78	$0.46	$6.24
Tuna	6 ounces	$0.89	14	$12.46	$1.00	$13.46
Apples	1 apple	$0.99	14	$13.86	$1.11	$14.97
Iced Tea	12 bottles	$9.99	2	$19.98	$1.60	$21.58
Frozen Dinners	1 box	$4.29	14	$60.06	$4.80	$64.86
Ice Cream Bars	8 bars	$3.49	2	$6.98	$0.56	$7.54
					Grand Total	$145.43

1. Yes. The grand total was $145.43 and we had $150.
2. We have enough.
3. Subtract: $150 – $145.43 = $4.57

(A) **Answers for Explore:**

Fractions in the Decimal Places

1. $\dfrac{7}{10}$

2. $\dfrac{9}{100}$

3. 0.09

4. It's like dividing by 1,000. $1 \div 1,000 = 0.001$

5. $\dfrac{2}{1000}$

6. $\dfrac{1}{10,000}$

Adding and Subtracting Decimals

$32.35 + 25.72 = 58.07$

$32.35 - 25.72 = 6.63$

Percents

We see percents everywhere, especially when we're purchasing items. A shirt is on sale for 20% off. A tip is often 15%. There was a 5% price increase on shoes you wanted, so you can't afford them anymore. **Percent** means "divided by 100." A percent is also sometimes referred to as a **percentage**.

At the end of this lesson, you will be able to:

- convert fractions and decimals into percents

- convert percents into fractions and decimals

- find percents of a number

Parent's Corner

A percent is a value out of 100. Start to remind students about the relationship between decimals and percents. If you see the decimal 0.75, think about how that can be expressed as a percent (75%) and vice versa. Get students thinking in terms of percents: if you have a collection of 10 books, ask your student what percent of the books the student has already read.

Dive Right In!

Percents and Nutrition

Directions: Read the information below and answer the questions.

Sample Label for Macaroni & Cheese			
Nutrition Facts			
Serving Size 1 cup (228g)			
Servings Per Container 2			
Amount Per Serving			
Calories 250		Calories from Fat 110	
		% Daily Value*	
Total Fat 12g		18%	
Saturated Fat 3g		15%	
Trans Fat 3g			
Cholesterol 30mg		10%	
Sodium 470mg		20%	
Total Carbohydrate 31g		10%	
Dietary Fiber 0g		0%	
Sugars 5g			
Protein 5g			
Vitamin A		4%	
Vitamin C		2%	
Calcium		20%	
Iron		4%	

* Percent Daily Values are based on a 2,000 calorie diet. Your Daily Values may be higher or lower depending on your calorie needs.

	Calories:	2,000	2,500
Total Fat	Less than	65g	80g
Sat Fat	Less than	20g	25g
Cholesterol	Less than	300mg	300mg
Sodium	Less than	2,400mg	2,400mg
Total Carbohydrate		300g	375g
Dietary Fiber		25g	30g

1. A serving of Macaroni & Cheese provides 12g of fat, which is 18% of your fat intake for the day. How many grams of fat would be 100% of your daily intake?

2. How many grams of saturated fat would be 100% of your daily intake?

3. How many carbohydrates does the average person need every day, according to the label?

4. How many servings of Macaroni & Cheese would you need to eat to get your recommended daily value of iron?

5. What about calcium?

Answers can be found on page 260.

 **Explore**

Conversions

In order to work with percents, you need to convert them to either fractions or decimals. You can't combine numbers that aren't in the same form.

Percent to Decimal

Because a percent is part of 100, we can convert percents to decimals by taking off the percent sign and moving the decimal to the left 2 places.

1. How would you change 75% to a decimal?

Decimal to Percent

In order to convert decimals to percents, multiply the decimal by 100, or move the decimal 2 places to the right. Both of these actions accomplish the same thing. Don't forget to add a percent sign.

2. How would you change 0.19 to a percent?

Percent to Fraction

Remember that a percent just means "a number divided by 100." Mathematically this can be written as $\frac{n}{100}$. So if you have to convert 55% to a fraction, put the number over 100 and simplify.

3. How would 55% be represented as a fraction?

Fraction to Percent

In order to convert a fraction to a percent, first convert the fraction to a decimal. Then, use what you just learned to convert the decimal to a fraction.

4. How would you write $\dfrac{3}{25}$ as a percent?

Finding Percents of Numbers

Finding the percent of a number means that you're finding some part of a whole.

5. Let's say that you want to buy a new bicycle and you notice that the bike store is having a sale. The bicycle you want usually costs $200, but the store is offering a 30% discount. How much money will you save? In other words, what is 30% of $200?

Remember that when translating English into math, *of* means multiply.

So the question above would be translated as follows:

$$0.30 \times 200$$

The answer is 60. So 30% of $200 is $60, which means you would save $60 if you bought the bicycle during the sale.

There is another way to figure out this problem. Remember that *percent* means "divided by 100." Therefore, you might come up with another equation:

$$\frac{30}{100} \times 200 = 60$$

So you see that the problem can be done either by converting to a decimal or to a fraction. Both methods give you the same answer.

6. You can take the question one step further and figure out how much you'd pay for the bike. How would you do that?

Answers can be found on page 260.

Percents and Word Problems

We talked about finding a percent of a certain number. Now we're going to use this method to solve a word problem that contains a percent.

7. A music store is offering 20% off all music. You want to buy a double album that normally costs $25. How much would you pay for the double album?

First, translate the problem into a question that you can understand. The first question is: What is 20% of $25?

Now translate the question to math. The math problem becomes

$$20\% \times 25 = x$$

Because you can't multiply numbers and percents together, change the percent into a decimal or a fraction before you simplify.

$$0.2 \times 25 = x$$

$$5 = x$$

Are you done? Did we answer the question? No. In order to find out how much you'd pay for the album, subtract the amount you'd save from the original price. You'd pay $20 for the book.

Let's look at another type of word problem.

8. In a class of 24 students, 6 students were absent. What percent of the students were absent?

This question asks you to find a percent. First, translate the question into math. When trying to find a percent, using fractions is often easier than using decimals. Remember that percent means $\dfrac{x}{100}$.

$$\frac{x}{100} \times 24 = 6$$

Now all you have to do is solve: $x = 25$. So 25% of the students were absent.

ONE MORE THING... Understanding percents helps us function in our world every day. They are used in stores, in polling surveys, to measure test scores, and much more. Not only do stores use percents to offer sales on certain items, but many states also charge a sales tax on most items—usually between 4% and 10% of the purchase price.

Participate

Activity: Hands-On

Go into the cupboard and find 3 more nutrition labels to analyze.
Look at the % daily value total and convert those to fractions.

In a Nutshell

Definition

- **Percent:** expressing something as divided by 100, sometimes called a percentage

Rules

- To convert percents to decimals, remove the percent sign and move the decimal to the left 2 places.

- To convert decimals to percents, multiply the decimal by 100, or move the decimal 2 places to the right.

Answers for Dive Right In:

1. Translate: $\dfrac{5}{27}$. This simplifies to approximately 67 g.
2. Translate again: $\dfrac{27}{27} - \dfrac{5}{27} = \dfrac{22}{27}$. This simplifies to 20 g.
3. More translation. See if students see a shortcut to it (If 31 g is 10%, then 310 g is 100%). If they don't see it, have them write it out. 310 g
4. How do you get from 4% to 100%? Multiply by 25. So the answer is 25 servings.
5. How do you get from 20% to 100%? Multiply by 5. The answer is 5 servings.

Answers for Explore:

Percent to Decimal

1. 0.75

Decimal to Percent

2. 19%

Percent to Fraction

3. $\dfrac{11}{20}$

Fraction to Percent

4. 12%

Finding Percents of Numbers

6. Subtract 60 from the total, 200 – 60 = $140 the cost of the bike.

   (5., 7., and 8. are answered within the text.)

Mean

The **mean** is an average. In this chapter, you will learn how to find the mean of a list of numbers. Sometimes, a list of numbers is called a **set** if there are no repeating numbers in the list. You will also see how different statistics can influence people's views.

At the end of this lesson, you will be able to:

- identify the mean of a set of numbers

- practice finding the average of two numbers

- select the best statistic to make an argument about a set of numbers

Parent's Corner

Although the technical term is "arithmetic mean," you can think of a "mean" as an "average." Do make sure that your fifth grader understands that "mean" and "average" are the same concept.

Dive Right In!

Putting Statistics to Use

Directions: A magazine surveyed people across the country to determine the success of different dating trends. Here are the results of their research. Read the below chart and answer the questions.

Dating Format	Number Who Have Tried It	Number Who Were Successful*
Speed Dating	11	2
Online Dating—App	72	5
Online Date—Website	20	3
Blind Dating	45	5
Matchmaking Service	7	5

Successful is defined as going out on 3 or more dates with a person.

1. What is the mean of people who were successful with their dating method?

2. What is the mean number of people who were not successful with their dating method?

Answers can be found on page 266.

Explore

Mean

Mean is the *average* of a set of numbers. Sometimes you will see it called the **arithmetic mean**. You can find the mean of a set of numbers by adding up all the numbers in the set and dividing the total by how many numbers you have. Finding the average is the "mean" one; that is, it requires the most work. Let's try one.

List *Z*: {14, 33, 7, 21, 5}

The first thing you need to do when finding the mean of a set of numbers is to add all the numbers up. Even though the numbers are in a list from side to side, you'll want to write them in a list up and down so that you can add them easily.

1. What is the total sum of the numbers?

2. Now that you have the sum, the next step is to divide the sum by the number of things you had to add up. In this case, we added five numbers, so we need to divide 80 by 5. What do you get?

Answers can be found on page 266.

The sum of all the numbers divided by how many numbers you have gives you your average.

Participate

Activity: Hands-On

Look at the newspaper and see the temperatures listed for the week. What is the range of temperatures shown? What is the mean temperature?

In a Nutshell

Definition

- **Mean:** the average of a set of numbers, sometimes called the arithmetic mean; it's found by adding up the numbers in a list and dividing by how many numbers you have

Answers for Dive Right In:

1. 4

2. This set is not on the chart above. You have to find it. Number tried it − Number successful = Number not successful. For example, to find the speed dating entry, 11 − 2 = 9 people who were unsuccessful with speed dating. From top to bottom, those numbers would be 9, 67, 17, 40, 2; The mean is 27.

 Answers for Explore:

1. 80

2. 16

Distance, Rate, and Time Problems

H ow do you decide how much time to leave yourself to get to school in the morning? About how long does it take you to get to the store? What time do you get up in the morning? Why?

At the end of this lesson, you will be able to:

- understand and use the distance formula

- use the distance formula to answer rate problems

- use the distance formula to answer motion problems

Parent's Corner

Make sure to reiterate the formula: distance = rate × time ($d = rt$; "dirt" is a fun way to remember it!) Make car rides educational: If Boston is 121 miles away, and we are driving at 60 miles per hour, about how many hours will it take to get to Boston? Remind students how useful math can be for real-life scenarios!

Dive Right In!

Marvelous Marathon

Directions: The television show "Marvelous Marathon" shows crazy racers racing for a prize. The first over the finish line wins! This week features a man in a hang glider, a rider and his camel, and a man wearing gas-powered jumping shoes. The hang glider flies at 30 mph, the camel gallops at 18 mph, and the jumping shoes will propel the runner at 15 mph. The marathon is 26 miles long.

1. If it takes the hang glider 1 hour to get to a mountaintop high enough to use his hang glider, thus giving the other 2 racers a 1 hour head start, who will come in first?

2. Who will come in second?

3. If the camel rider has to stop and rest for 20 minutes midway through the race, what order will the racers reach the finish line? Assume that the hang glider still takes 1 hour to get to the top of the mountain to begin the race.

Answers can be found on page 274.

 **Explore**

The Distance Formula

Time, space, and speed are all related. You can see how they connect in the following problem.

1. Joe bikes to school every day. He bikes 20 miles per hour. It takes him 30 minutes to get to school. How far does Joe live from school?

    a. What do you know?

    b. How many miles is the trip?

    c. How did you figure that out?

Here is the distance formula. If you know two of the three variables, you can figure the other one out.

$$\textbf{distance} = \textbf{rate} \times \textbf{time}$$

or

$$d = rt$$

"**Dirt**" is a good mnemonic device to help you remember this formula.

Solve for Rate

Think about when you're riding in a car. The car has a speedometer. The speedometer usually displays the speed in terms of mph, which stands for *miles per hour*. This is an average speed. **Rate** means average speed, often talked about in miles per hour or kilometers per hour.

Let's review averages for a moment. To find the mean, or average, of a group of numbers, you add them up and then divide by how many numbers there are.

2. Look at the following set of numbers: {3, 7, 5, 2, 1, 6}.

   a. What's the total when you add up these numbers?

   b. How many numbers are in the set?

   c. What's the mean?

So, to find the average you find the total and divide by the number of things.

Try this problem.

3. A boat departs from Port Alexia at 10 A.M. and arrives at Port Ulysses at 4 P.M. The boat traveled 480 miles from port to port without stopping. What was the rate of the boat?

   a. Let's take this step by step. First, what's the total distance?

   b. How much time did it take?

   c. Use the formula to figure out the rate (average speed).

Solving for Time

Now let's shuffle things around a bit. What if you knew the rate and distance but you didn't know the time?

Take a look at this problem.

4. Juan must drive 360 miles to his cousin's house. He drives 60 miles an hour. How long will it take him to get there?

   a. What was the original formula?

   b. Fill in what you know and solve for the remaining variable.

Answers can be found on page 274.

ONE MORE THING...

Airlines depend on rate, time, and distance in order to create their schedules and their flight plans. It would be pretty hard to even approximate how much time a trip takes without knowing how fast you are going and the distance you have to travel. When pilots are flying through storms and have to reduce their speeds, the airline can do the appropriate calculation to figure out the new time it will take to arrive and inform people how late the flight will be.

 **Participate**

Activity: Hands-On

Think of a specific trip: it could be the bus ride to school or subway ride to a place or car ride to the store. How long did that trip take? How far were you going? Using what you learned in the "Solve for Rate" section of the chapter, calculate how fast you were going on that trip.

In a Nutshell

Definitions

- **Distance:** how far a thing travels

- **Rate:** the speed at which a thing travels

Hint

- For long problems, remember to write everything out.

Rule

- distance = rate × time or $d = rt$.

Answers for Dive Right In:

1. The hang glider takes .86 hours, but have to add an hour on for a total of 1.86 hours, the camel rider will take 1.44 hours total; and the runner will take 1.73 hours. The camel rider wins.

2. From what we figured out in Question 1, the runner.

3. The camel rider initially took about 1.44 hours. 20 minutes is $\frac{1}{3}$ of an hour, or .33 hour. If we add .33 to 1.44, we find that it took the camel rider 1.77 hours, which is longer than the runner's time. The runner comes in first, then the camel rider, and then the glider.

 Answers for Explore:

1. a. How fast Joe can bike (Joe's rate), and how long the trip took

   b. 10

   c. by multiplying 20 miles per hour $\times \dfrac{30}{60}$ hours

2. a. 24

   b. 6

   c. 4

3. a. 480 miles

   b. 6 hours

   c. 80 mph

4. a. *distance = rate × time*

   b. *360 = 60 × time; time = 6 hours*

Money Problems

Money, for better or for worse, is one of the most important things in our lives, so you can understand why finding the cost of items is important.

At the end of this lesson, you will be able to:

- use the cost formula to find the price, quantity, and cost of items
- use percent sales such as taxes and discounts with the cost formula

Parent's Corner

Think about how you can relate concepts of money math to your student's life. Do you have a set of bills or receipts you can show to your child? When the check comes at a restaurant, ask your child to figure out how much each person owes toward the total?

Dive Right In!

Financing a Fencing Club

Directions: You've always liked swords, so you are starting a fencing club at school. After speaking with your coaches, you have come up with a list of supplies that you will need for each club member.

Supplies to Buy	
Fencing jackets	$60/each
Gloves	$11.95/set
Mask	$54/each
Chest guard	$29.95/each
Practice foil	$23/each

The school will give your club $250, and you have 12 people who are interested. That's not going to be enough money!

1. What is the total cost per fencer for a full fencing uniform (not including the foil)?

2. How much money do you need to raise for each member to have a full set of fencing equipment?

3. You decide to have a bake sale to defray some of the cost and you raise $850. How many full sets of fencing equipment could you buy with the total money you have now?

4. Is that enough? You speak to the owner of a fencing supply store and explain that you don't have much money but would really like to start a high school club. She says she can give you a 20% discount. How many members can you suit up now?

5. You explain the situation to the members and suggest that they pay yearly dues. They agree to pay $20 per year. How many sets can you buy now?

6. Can you think of any other ways the fencing club can cut costs and buy some more equipment?

Answers can be found on page 284.

Explore

Finding Cost

When you buy a tomato at a store, you look at the price, decide if you have enough money, and then buy it. However, let's say that your dog ran away one afternoon and came back really smelly. You realize that your dog has been attacked by a skunk! The only thing to remove the smell is tomato juice, and you need lots of it. How could you figure out how much multiple cans will cost altogether? That's what we're going to figure out! Let's make that tomato soup problem more specific.

1. A can of George's tomato soup costs $1.50, but you need 7 large cans to bathe your dog. How would you figure out how much money you need?

Once again, we can figure out the formula from the information we already know. The formula that you discovered is **cost = price × quantity.** To figure out the total cost, take the price of the item and multiply it by how many of them you're buying.

Let's look at another example.

2. At the U-Save Gas Station, gas costs $2.25 per gallon. Sally wants to purchase 20 gallons of gas for her truck. How much will Sally pay for gas?

In order to solve the problem, answer a series of questions.

     a.   What's the price?

     b.   What's the quantity?

     c.   What formula do you need?

     d.   How much will Sally pay for gas?

Finding Price

You can also use the cost formula to find price. Divide both sides of the equation by quantity so that you are solving for price.

$$\frac{\text{cost}}{\text{quantity}} = \text{price}$$

3. Now let's say you gave your friend $20 to go to the store and get cans of soup for you because you have to stay with your smelly dog. Your friend brings back $5 and 15 cans. How much did each can cost? How did you figure it out?

Let's try one more.

4. Carrie goes to Priced-2-Sell. She pays $25 for 10 pairs of flip-flops. How much did each pair cost?

   a.   What's the total cost?

   b.   How many items did she buy?

   c.   What's the price of each item?

Finding Quantity

That cost formula is very flexible! You can also use it to find quantity. Divide both sides of the original equation by price so you are solving for quantity.

$$\frac{\text{cost}}{\text{price}} = \text{quantity}$$

5. You saw a sale sign for Fresco brand cans of tomato soup and you know that they cost 75 cents each. You gave your friend $20 and sent him to the store to buy all the cans on the shelves. He comes back with $3.50. How many cans did he buy?

6. Marlene has to go to the bank to deposit money for work. The money is kept in different envelopes for different departments. She deposits $3,360. If each envelope holds $60, how many envelopes did she deposit?

Percent Sales

Percents add another element to your problem-solving process.

7. Now, let's say that the Camden's brand cans of soup are marked down 25% per can. Cans were originally $1. You know that you need 10 cans to fill up your tub. How would you figure out how much money it will cost?

Now there are more steps, but they are all steps you've done before.

Let's take another example.

8. Ramon goes to the shoe store. He wants a pair of sneakers that costs $200. They're marked down by 30%. How much does Ramon pay for the sneakers?

   a. We need to translate into math. What part of the question would you translate?

   b. Now translate and solve.

   c. Is that the answer to the question? Why or why not?

   d. If that's not the answer to the question, what is?

Challenge

Now let's get a little funky with percents. Look at the following question.

9. Jodi goes to a coat sale. She sees a coat on the sale rack. The rack says 25% off everything on it. The coat that she chooses was originally priced at $350, but on the tag has already been marked down 20%. What is the final price of the coat?

    a. Let's take this in steps. Write down the original price.

    b. What is the first thing that happens to that price? Translate and calculate this first step and show your work.

    c. What happens to the price next?

    d. Solve the next step. (Remember that you're starting with your new number here.)

    e. What's your final answer?

Answers can be found on pages 284–285.

 **ONE MORE THING...** Understanding cost and percents is extremely useful when you're buying things. You want to be able to figure out how much you're going to pay before you get to the cash register! If you only have $10 in your pocket, you don't want to wait on a really long line only to realize you don't have enough money when the cashier rings up your purchase.

Participate

Activity: Hands-On

Grab some paper, pencil, and a die (number cube). Roll the die four times. Each number that you rolled is a number in the total of your bank account. So, for example, if you rolled a 4 then an 8 then a 1 then a 6, your bank account total is $4,816. Make your rolls and write down those numbers.

You want to give some of your money to charity. Which charities will you donate to? How much will you give? How much money is left in your bank account now? What is one half, or 50%, of that?

In a Nutshell

Definitions

- **Cost:** the amount of money used in a purchase

- **Price:** the amount of money needed to buy an item

- **Quantity:** the number of items bought in a purchase

Hint

- For long problems, remember to write everything out and translate.

Rule

- Cost = Price × Quantity

Answers for Dive Right In:

1. $60 + $11.95 + $54 + $29.95 = $155.90

2. 1 full set = $155.90 + $23.00 for the foil = $178.90. 12($178.90) = $2,146.80 total. The school gives $250, so $2,146.80 − $250 = $1,896,80 left to raise.

3. $250 + $850 = $1,100.00. Now divide that by the cost of each set: $1,100 ÷ $178.90 ≈ 6.

4. 20% off $178.90 gives a price of about $143.12; $1,100.00 ÷ $143.12 ≈ 7.

5. 12 × $20 = $240; $240 + $1,100.00 = $1,340. Now divide that by the discounted price: $1,340 ÷ $143.12 ≈ 9.

6. Solicit the students for their ideas.

Answers for Explore:

1. $1.50 × 7 = $10.50

2. a. $2.25 per gallon

    b. 20 gallons

    c. $2.25 × 20

    d. $45

3. ($20 − $5) ÷ 15 = $1

4. a. $25

    b. 10

    c. $2.50

5. He bought $16.50 worth of soup. 16.50 ÷ 0.75 = 22 cans.

6. $3360 = $60 × q; q = 56.

7. The discount is = $\dfrac{25}{100}$ × $1.00, or 0.25. Take it from the original price to find the new price of 75 cents.

8. a. What is 30% of \$200?

   b. $x = \dfrac{30}{100} \times \$200; x = \$60$

   c. No, the question asked how much he paid, and we have only found the discount.

   d. \$140

9. a. The original price is \$350

   b. Take 20% off of \$350; $\dfrac{20}{100} \times \$350 = \$70; \$350 - \$70 = \$280$

   c. An additional 25% is taken off the price, so $\dfrac{25}{100} \times \$280 = \$70$; $\$280 - \$70 = \$210$

   d. \$210

Factors and Prime Numbers

If a number is a whole meal, then its "dishes" are the **factors**, and the very basic ingredients are called **prime numbers**.

A whole meal may be a really big number, and we can break it into separate courses—that is, smaller numbers. Each course and each number can be broken into smaller parts until we can't go any further.

Factoring breaks down large numbers into smaller, more useful building blocks. The smallest building blocks are **prime numbers**. In this section, you'll learn to factor with primes.

At the end of this lesson, you will be able to:

- learn to factor numbers

- recognize primes

- find the greatest common factor between two numbers

Parent's Corner

Know that prime numbers are special: they are numbers that have only two factors: themselves and 1. (The smallest prime number is 2.) Quiz your student on what makes a prime number a prime number. Can they name some prime numbers, like 2, 3, 5, 7? Help your student visualize breaking up larger numbers into their *prime factors* by drawing factor trees and hanging them up.

Dive Right In!

Complete the Trees

Directions: Complete the factor trees to find what smaller numbers can be multiplied to make the larger numbers on top of them. The numbers in the circles will be prime numbers because they can't be reduced any further.

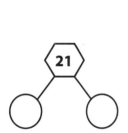

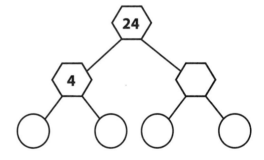

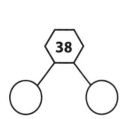

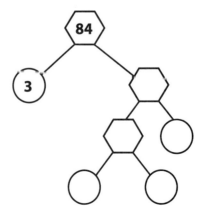

Answers can be found on page 295.

Explore

Factoring

Factoring (sometimes called **factorization**) is the process of listing all the ways we can make a number by multiplying different integers together. For example, how many different ways can we make 30?

$$1 \times 30 = 30$$

$$2 \times 15 = 30$$

$$3 \times 10 = 30$$

$$5 \times 6 = 30$$

We can write all of the factors in a factor list. Notice that each factor is only listed once.

Factor list: {1, 2, 3, 4, 5, 6, 10, 15, 30}

Helpful Tips for Factoring

- Make pairs. List only two numbers at a time, as we did above.
- Start with 1. Its partner is always the number you are factoring itself, which is a factor as well.
- Go in ascending order: try 2, then 3, 4, and so forth. Note that as our first factor of a pair gets bigger, our second factor gets smaller. Eventually, the two groups of numbers will meet in the middle, and you won't have to worry that you've missed any.

Prime Numbers

Prime numbers (also called **primes**) are the basic ingredients, like the tomatoes in a spaghetti dish. They are the numbers we can't break down any further into smaller parts. In math terms, we define them as whole numbers that can only be broken into two distinct factors, themselves and 1. For example, 3 is a prime number, because it can be broken down only into the factors 3 and 1. The number 1 is not a prime, because 1 and 1 are both the same factor—the factors are not different.

List the first 10 prime numbers.

Factoring with Prime Numbers

Every whole number greater than 1 is either a prime or is made up of different combinations of primes. So instead of listing all the different ways we can make a number, we want to break it down to nothing but its smallest parts, or prime numbers.

For example, let's find the prime factors of 420. What's the first step?

It looks even, so we divide it by 2, which is the smallest prime, and get two factors.

Because 2 is prime (it can't be divided any further), we're done on that side. How about 210? Let's divide by 2 again to check: We get 2 and 105. Continue the factor tree you started above.

What's next? 105 ends with a 5, so we should try dividing it by 5.

We're done with the two 2s and the 5. What about 21? It's not even, so can't be divisible by 2. It doesn't end in 5 or 0, so it isn't divisible by 5. Let's try 3.

Are we done? Can 3 or 7 be broken up into smaller parts? No. Like 2 and 5, they are both prime.

Breaking a number down to its prime numbers is called prime factoring (or prime factorization). Here is the prime factorization of 420:

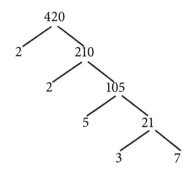

$$2 \times 2 \times 3 \times 5 \times 7 = 420$$

More Helpful Tips for Factoring

- It doesn't matter where you begin; you'll end up at the same place in the end.
- However, it's easiest to begin with one of the three smallest primes: 2, 3, and 5. (Remember, 1 is always a factor, but it is NOT a prime number.)
- If a number is even, it's divisible by 2.
- If a number ends in 5 or 0, it's divisible by 5.
- If the sum of the digits of a number is divisible by 3, the number itself is divisible by 3. For example, 2 + 1 = 3, which is divisible by 3. So 12 and 21 are both divisible by 3.
- Move on to the larger primes (7, 11, 13, 17, 19, 23) once you have exhausted the small ones.
- Stop when you are left with nothing but primes.

Greatest Common Factors

You may have noticed that the number 2 appears in a lot of the examples. When two or more numbers share a factor, that factor is called a **common factor**. For instance, 186 and 18 both have 2 as a factor, so it is a common factor for these numbers. They also share other factors, such as 1, 3, 6, 9, and 18.

Multiply all the prime common factors together to find the **greatest common factor**. Let's look at another example. Find the prime factors of 30 and 45 separately.

$$30 \rightarrow (2, \mathbf{3}, \mathbf{5})$$

$$45 \rightarrow (3, \mathbf{3}, \mathbf{5})$$

Both 30 and 45 have 3 and 5 as common factors. When multiplied together, $3 \times 5 = 15$. Therefore, 15 is the **greatest common factor** (or **GCF**) of 30 and 45.

 Factoring is very useful in school. For example, dividing numerators and denominators by the same prime number can help you reduce a fraction to its lowest common form quickly.

Prime numbers also excite cryptologists, people who create and decipher codes for a living. Really large prime numbers are hard to figure out and make factoring, or code-breaking, more difficult. Online stores and banks use a complex system of coded primes to hide your personal information on the Internet.

Participate

Activity: Hands-On

This activity should be done with a friend or sibling. Sit across from each other and go back and forth, taking turns, reciting the first 10 prime numbers. Then, on a piece of paper, factor the number 1050 by breaking it down, step by step as we learned in the chapter.

In a Nutshell

Definitions

- **Factor:** a whole number that divides into another number without leaving a remainder; for instance, 3 is a factor of 6

- **Prime Number:** a number that only has 1 and itself as factors; for example, 7 is prime

- **Factoring:** breaking down larger numbers into their prime factors, sometimes called factorization

- **Common Factor:** a factor shared by 2 or more numbers

- **Greatest Common Factor:** the largest factor shared by 2 or more numbers

Hints

- Make Pairs: When factoring, list only 2 numbers at a time.

- Go in Ascending Order: try 2, then 3, 4, and so on. Note that as our first factor of a pair gets bigger, our second factor gets smaller. Eventually, you will meet in the middle, and you won't have to worry that you've missed any.

Answers for Dive Right In:

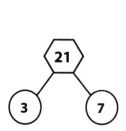

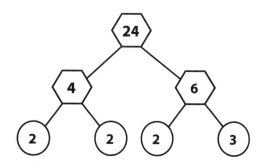

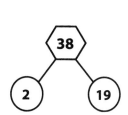

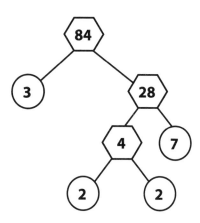

NOTES

NOTES

NOTES